SPHR
Exam
Practice Questions

SPHR Practice Tests & Review for the
Senior Professional in Human
Resources Certification Exam

Reporting
Program.

Dear Future Exam Success Story:

First of all, **THANK YOU** for purchasing Mometrix study materials!

Second, congratulations! You are one of the few determined test-takers who are committed to doing whatever it takes to excel on your exam. **You have come to the right place.** We developed these practice tests with one goal in mind: to deliver you the best possible approximation of the questions you will see on test day.

Standardized testing is one of the biggest obstacles on your road to success, which only increases the importance of doing well in the high-pressure, high-stakes environment of test day. Your results on this test could have a significant impact on your future, and these practice tests will give you the repetitions you need to build your familiarity and confidence with the test content and format to help you achieve your full potential on test day.

Your success is our success

We would love to hear from you! If you would like to share the story of your exam success or if you have any questions or comments in regard to our products, please contact us at **800-673-8175** or **support@mometrix.com**.

Thanks again for your business and we wish you continued success!

Sincerely,
The Mometrix Test Preparation Team

TABLE OF CONTENTS

Practice Test #1

1. To qualify for an H-1B visa allowing him to come to America on a temporary basis to work in a specialty occupation, a foreign worker would need the equivalent of a:

    a. Doctoral degree
    b. Master's degree
    c. Bachelor's degree
    d. High school diploma

2. In which business structure do partners exist mainly as investors, without much influence on daily operations?

    a. limited liability partnership
    b. sole proprietorship
    c. general partnership
    d. joint venture

3. Which piece of legislation declared that back pay awards cannot be a part of compensatory damages?

    a. Civil Rights Act of 1964
    b. Civil Rights Act of 1991
    c. Equal Employment Opportunity Act of 1974
    d. Americans with Disabilities Act of 1990

4. The SMART model outlines the important characteristics of

    a. forecasting studies.
    b. employee training.
    c. effective recruiting.
    d. organizational goals.

5. Name one consequence of the Clayton Act of 1914.

    a. Workers retained the right to organize.
    b. The Sherman Act was applied to unions.
    c. Employers could not always use injunctions to break strikes.
    d. Federal contractors must pay the going rate for workers.

6. Which of the following statements about performance appraisal is false?

    a. Ranking is a good method for appraising large groups of employees.
    b. Focal review programs include all of the employees in an organization.
    c. Forced ranking systems assume that most employees are neither exceptionally good nor exceptionally bad.
    d. A behaviorally anchored rating system isolates each job's most important tasks.

7. Which of the following would be considered nonmonetary compensation?

    a. flex time
    b. stock options
    c. medical care premiums
    d. paid leave

8. Which piece of legislation established a new definition for "highly compensated individual"?

    a. Small Business Regulatory Enforcement Act Fairness Act of 1996
    b. Sarbanes-Oxley Act of 2002
    c. Small Business Job Protection Act of 1996
    d. Pension Protection Act of 2006

9. In business, what is the primary difference between a goal and a strategy?

    a. The terms are interchangeable.
    b. Strategies are created by executives, while goals are set by middle managers.
    c. Strategies precede goals.
    d. Strategies are the means, while goals are the end.

10. A new employee is told by her coworkers that one of her duties is to handle customer queries as they arrive. However, her superior informs her that customer queries are to be handled by her department as a whole, and in fact she should defer to her coworkers until she becomes more acclimated. This employee's situation can be defined as

    a. role orientation.
    b. role conflict.
    c. role overload.
    d. role ambiguity.

11. Which of the following institutions did not receive Title VII coverage pursuant to the Equal Employment Opportunity Act of 1972?

    a. Religious institutions
    b. Universities
    c. State government agencies
    d. Federal legislative bodies

12. Which of the following is an example of a chemical health hazard?

    a. bacterium
    b. pesticide
    c. fungus
    d. virus

13. The Stanley Corporation wants to avoid lawsuits, so the human resources department occasionally reviews the hiring process to ensure compliance with all equal opportunity regulations. This is an example of

    a. risk avoidance.
    b. risk elimination.
    c. risk mitigation.
    d. risk transfer.

14. Which of the following was a consequence of the Workforce Investment Act?

    a. A Mass layoff was defined as either 500 employees or 33% of workforce.
    b. Workers must be given 60 days notice before plant closing.
    c. Labor unions were encouraged to cooperate with management on worker training.
    d. The creation of comprehensive training centers for workers and employers

15. According to Edward E. Lawler, the four elements of a high-involvement organization are
	a. knowledge, communication, incentives, and evaluation.
	b. planning, execution, evaluation, and control.
	c. selection, maintenance, evaluation, and forecasting.
	d. power, information, knowledge, and rewards.

16. Which of the following statements about union decertification is true?
	a. Decertification does not prevent employees from joining a different union later.
	b. Decertification only occurs when employees are displeased with the union.
	c. Employers may lobby employees during the decertification process.
	d. Half the employees must petition the NLRB before a decertification vote is held.

17. In which case did the Fifth Circuit determine that a company may not claim physical difficulty as a bona fide occupational qualification in order to keep women out of certain jobs?
	a. Rosenfeld v. Southern Pacific (1968)
	b. McDonnell Douglas Corporation v. Green (1973)
	c. Weeks v. Southern Bell Telephone Company (1969)
	d. Texas *Department of Community Affairs v. Burdine* (1981)

18. Which component of an affirmative action plan provides demographic information for the labor market related to each job group?
	a. job group analysis
	b. determination of availability
	c. comparison of incumbency to availability
	d. organizational profile

19. What is one common problem with cost-per-hire metrics?
	a. They make no distinctions between job groups.
	b. They are overly dependent on external economic factors.
	c. They overemphasize advertising.
	d. They omit costs that are not related to specific candidates.

20. A new employee enters the training room and notices that the seats have been arranged in a banquet style. What can the new employee expect to do during the training session?
	a. Work in a small group
	b. Watch a video
	c. Take notes
	d. Fill out a questionnaire

21. Ron and Marcy apply for the same job at the Brown Company. During Ron's interview, the interviewer outlines the major responsibilities of the available position, and asks Ron a series of questions about his ability to fulfill them. Marcy's interview covers much of the same ground, but the interviewer asks different questions related to Marcy's unique educational background. Ron and Marcy have participated in
	a. structured interviews.
	b. stress interviews.
	c. patterned interviews.
	d. nondirective interviews

22. Which of the following statements about strikes is false?

    a. Unions may not strike in favor of an unfair labor practice.
    b. Work slowdowns are an illegal form of strike.
    c. Employees may strike to support a hot cargo clause.
    d. A strike may be deemed unlawful because of misconduct by strikers.

23. The orientation program at Company X is considered very intense. New employees are given a crash course in organizational philosophy, and are discouraged from voicing their opinions or concerns. Which type of people processing strategy is Company X using?

    a. investiture
    b. contest
    c. collective
    d. divestiture

24. Which piece of legislation forbade yellow dog contracts?

    a. Fair Labor Standards Act of 1938
    b. Norris-LaGuardia Act of 1932
    c. Public Contracts Act of 1936
    d. Sherman Anti-Trust Act of 1890

25. The human resources department wants to see if experienced employees are more productive. The department takes a measure of each employee's productivity, and then plots it on a graph, on which the other axis is employee experience. Which correlation coefficient would be the strongest suggestion that productivity increases with experience?

    a. +0.8
    b. +0.2
    c. 0
    d. -0.9

26. Which of the following statements about drug testing programs is true?

    a. Scheduled drug testing programs are the most effective.
    b. Businesses must either test all or no job candidates.
    c. Businesses can decide to test certain job groups only.
    d. Candidates may be drug tested before an offer of employment has been made.

27. Summarize the ruling in *Regents of California v. Bakke* (1978).

    a. Nonunion employees are not entitled to Weingarten rights.
    b. Arbitration clauses are enforceable even when a business is engaged in interstate commerce.
    c. Employees must be given a reasonable opportunity to reject unfair arbitration clauses.
    d. Universities may not use quotas to boost minority admissions.

28. Which approach to budgeting requires that every expense be justified?

    a. historical budgeting
    b. parallel budgeting
    c. zero-based budgeting
    d. bottom-up budgeting

29. An employee's performance on an assembly line is likely to follow a

    a. negatively accelerating learning curve.
    b. proportionally accelerating learning curve.
    c. positively accelerating learning curve.
    d. statically accelerating learning curve.

30. Which of the following is NOT defined as a major life activity by the Americans with Disabilities Act?

    a. personal hygiene
    b. driving
    c. reading
    d. sleeping

31. The Archibald Corporation has offices in thirteen countries besides the United States. In these foreign offices, the management positions are held by locals and the corporate positions are held by Americans. What is one possible drawback of this arrangement?

    a. Organizational culture is too homogenous
    b. Resentment by the foreign community
    c. Lack of communication among the foreign offices
    d. Exaggerated hiring costs

32. How many weeks of unpaid leave is an employer required to give a new mother under the Family Medical Leave Act of 1993?

    a. 3
    b. 12
    c. 16
    d. 52

33. Which type of medical insurance plan makes contract arrangements directly with employers?

    a. health maintenance organization
    b. physician hospital organization
    c. preferred provider organization
    d. fee-for-service plan

34. The Williamson Company is using the paired comparison method to appraise performance. There are seven people in the sales job group. With how many people will each member of this group be compared?

    a. One
    b. Two
    c. Six
    d. Seven

35. What are Philip B. Crosby's four absolutes of quality?

    a. communication, recruiting, evaluation, and planning
    b. unfreezing, moving, refreezing, and evaluating
    c. team learning, systems thinking, personal mastery, and shared vision
    d. conformance to requirements, prevention, performance standards, and measurement

36. In Alderfer's theory of motivation, what do the letters ERG stand for?

    a. energy, relatedness, and growth
    b. existence, responsibility, and growth
    c. energy, responsibility, and growth
    d. existence, relatedness, and growth

37. In which case did the Supreme Court rule that contagious diseases should be treated as handicaps under Section 504 of the Rehabilitation Act?

    a. Martin v. Wilks (1989)
    b. Johnson v. Santa Clara County Transportation Agency (1987)
    c. School Board of Nassau v. Arline (1987)
    d. St. Mary's *Honor Center v. Hicks* (1993)

38. Which analytical tool indicates the changes that would produce the greatest improvement?

    a. histogram
    b. Pareto chart
    c. stratification chart
    d. Ishikawa diagram

39. The Henderson Company needs to hire a large number of unskilled employees to perform data entry. Which type of application would be most appropriate?

    a. long-form employment application
    b. short-form employment application
    c. weighted employment application
    d. job-specific employment application

40. A labor union must deal with several different employers. The union decides to negotiate with the employers one at a time, hoping to achieve successively better deals. What strategy is this union using?

    a. parallel bargaining
    b. integrative bargaining
    c. positional bargaining
    d. multi-unit bargaining

41. What is the name for the tendency to assign more responsibility for negative behavior to personality or effort rather than to environment?

    a. nonverbal bias
    b. fundamental attribution error
    c. recency bias
    d. halo effect

42. Dennis owns a small business. He is contacted by state law enforcement officials because one of his employees is delinquent in his child support payments. Which piece of legislation governs Dennis' conduct in this situation?

    a. Small Business Regulatory Enforcement Fairness Act of 1996
    b. Small Business Job Protection Act of 1996
    c. Privacy Act of 1974
    d. Personal Responsibility and Work Opportunity Reconciliation Act of 1996

43. How do corporations fund business operations?

    a. Bank loans
    b. Investments by partners
    c. Government subsidies
    d. Sale of stock

44. Which case first defined *employment at-will*?

    a. Payne v. The Western & Atlantic Railroad Company (1884)
    b. Burlington Industries v. Ellerth (1998)
    c. Albemarle Paper v. Moody (1975)
    d. Griggs *v. Duke Power* (1971)

45. The point factor method is used to

    a. ensure compliance with OSHA regulations.
    b. identify the most important positions in an organization.
    c. create fair performance incentives.
    d. incentivize waste elimination.

46. After his wife gives birth to their first child, Brian takes four weeks of FMLA leave. These are the only days of work Brian misses during the year. At the end of the year, his boss tells him that he is not eligible for a bonus given to employees who have not missed any days of work. However, his coworker Jill receives the bonus, and she had three days of paid leave after her mother died during the summer. Brian believes this is unfair and that he should receive the bonus too. Does he have a legitimate complaint?

    a. No, FMLA leave is counted differently than other forms of leave.
    b. No, neither Brian nor Jill should receive the bonus.
    c. Yes, FMLA leave should be treated the same as other forms of leave.
    d. Yes, Brain should receive the bonus, but Jill should not.

47. ERISA mandates that employees who use grade vesting must be fully vested in a qualified plan

    a. immediately.
    b. within four years.
    c. within seven years.
    d. before being laid off.

48. The salesmen at Franklin Company earn bonuses of $500, $750, $1000, $1000, and $1500, respectively. What is the median bonus?

    a. $500
    b. $950
    c. $1000
    d. $4750

49. During which phase of the strategic planning process would a SWOT analysis be most useful?

    a. evaluation
    b. environmental scan
    c. construction
    d. adjustment

50. Which of the following organizations must complete an annual EEO survey?

   a. A bank that issues United States savings bonds
   b. A university
   c. A local government with fewer than a hundred employees
   d. A federal subcontractor with more than a hundred employees

51. Which of the following is closest to the national LWDI average for private-sector organizations?

   a. 250
   b. 25
   c. 2.5
   d. 0.25

52. Which of the following correlation coefficients would indicate the strongest relationship between two variables?

   a. +0.7
   b. 0
   c. -0.1
   d. -0.9

53. What was the primary directive of the Worker Adjustment and Retraining Notification Act?

   a. Employers must submit planned expansions to an employee vote.
   b. Displaced workers must be given assistance in relocating.
   c. The unemployed must have access to training programs.
   d. Employees and unions must be notified in advance about planned plant closings.

54. Vince is a middle manager at Foster Company. He earns a base salary of $80,000, and the midpoint of the salary range for middle managers is $100,000. What is Vince's compa-ratio?

   a. 80%
   b. 100%
   c. 125%
   d. 180%

55. In which case did the Supreme Court rule that employee selection tools that adversely impact a protected class could still be legal if the employer can prove that the tool is predictive of success?

   a. Taxman v. Board of Education of Piscataway (1993)
   b. Automobile Workers v. Johnson Controls, Inc. (1977)
   c. Harris v. Forklift Systems (1993)
   d. Washington *v. Davis* (1976)

56. A Scanlon Plan is an example of a(n)

   a. individual incentive.
   b. sales bonus.
   c. group incentive.
   d. Employee Stock Ownership Plan.

57. For human resources departments, what is the first step in enterprise risk management?

    a. audit
    b. insurance
    c. forecasting
    d. employee interviews

58. Which of the following employees would be most likely to receive on-call pay?

    a. Dermatologist
    b. High school janitor with the keys to the school's generator
    c. Receptionist
    d. Police officer

59. Which type of strike is launched despite a no-strike clause in the employee contract?

    a. sit-down strike
    b. secondary strike
    c. hot cargo strike
    d. wildcat strike

60. Yolanda is a human resources officer at an accounting firm. During tax season, Yolanda contracts with an agency that supplies temporary workers. These workers are paid by the temp agency rather than the accounting firm. What type of contract will Yolanda sign with the temp agency?

    a. temporary contract
    b. resolvable contract
    c. third-party contract
    d. indirect contract

61. Which piece of federal legislation made it illegal to discharge an employee after only one garnishment order?

    a. Consumer Credit Protection Act of 1968
    b. Fair Credit Reporting Act of 1970
    c. Labor-Management Reporting and Disclosure Act of 1959
    d. Equal Pay Act of 1963

62. Fran is interviewing candidates for an accounting position. Glenda seems like a very qualified candidate, but Fran finds her voice very annoying. Despite Glenda's solid record, Fran hires another candidate. Fran's decision demonstrates the

    a. central tendency.
    b. horn effect.
    c. stereotyping bias.
    d. cultural noise bias.

63. Which term refers to employees of multinational corporations who hail from neither the home country of the corporation nor the location where they're actually working?

    a. Guest workers
    b. Third-country nationals
    c. Inpatriates
    d. Class C employees

64. Which of the following is NOT a chart commonly used in total quality management?

    a. Pareto chart
    b. pie chart
    c. scattergram
    d. histogram

65. Which of the following is an example of bottom-up communication?

    a. brown-bag lunch
    b. poster
    c. newsletter
    d. intranet

66. Programs that help union members maintain their skills and competence in their field are called

    a. adult recertification.
    b. corporate universities.
    c. continuing education.
    d. joint training programs.

67. Which of the following statements about the Delphi technique is false?

    a. The participants remain anonymous.
    b. It takes place in a single round.
    c. It is a convenient form of qualitative analysis when participants are distant.
    d. It allows for a broad range of perspectives.

68. A mid-range plan can be executed in

    a. six months.
    b. nine months.
    c. two years.
    d. four years.

69. At Danielson Company, the Monday after Labor Day is a paid holiday. Steve, an employee at Danielson Company, works nine-hour days on Tuesday, Wednesday, Thursday, Friday, and Saturday of that week. How many hours of overtime has Steve worked?

    a. None
    b. Five
    c. Nine
    d. Thirteen

70. Fernando shows up for work on Monday morning, but the office has been overstaffed, so his boss sends him home almost immediately. The compensation owed to Fernando is called

    a. on-call pay.
    b. call-back pay.
    c. reporting pay.
    d. shift pay.

- 10 -

71. What is the primary directive of the Federal Employees Compensation Act of 1916?

    a. To allocate funds to federal workers injured while performing their jobs
    b. To provide worker's compensation rights to employees in the private sector
    c. To guarantee a minimum wage to federal employees
    d. To outlaw the fellow servant rule

72. A human resources officer at a rapidly growing company is interviewing candidates for a position that has just been created. Management is not yet sure what the precise duties of the new employee will be, but it is very important for the new employee to fit into the organizational culture. What type of interview should the human resources officer conduct?

    a. directive interview
    b. panel interview
    c. stress interview
    d. nondirective interview

73. Which piece of legislation established that employees may not demand payment for their commute time?

    a. Fair Labor Standards Act
    b. Davis Bacon Act
    c. Portal to Portal Act
    d. Commute Compensation Act

74. What are the typical hours of the swing shift?

    a. 10 p.m. to 6 a.m.
    b. 12 a.m. to 8 a.m.
    c. 4 p.m. to 12 a.m.
    d. 5 p.m. to 1 a.m.

75. What is the largest possible damage award under the Civil Rights Act of 1991?

    a. $50,000
    b. $100,000
    c. $200,000
    d. $300,000

76. Which of the following is NOT part of Kirkpatrick's training evaluation framework?

    a. reaction
    b. results
    c. context
    d. learning

77. During the holiday season, Marsha works 30 hours of overtime. Her employer elects to give her compensatory time off instead of direct pay. How many hours of comp time has Marsha earned?

    a. 15 hours
    b. 20 hours
    c. 30 hours
    d. 45 hours

78. Tara's boss asks her to pick up an important client from the airport. The client's flight is delayed, so Tara goes to a nearby restaurant and eats dinner. Should Tara be compensated for this time?

    a. Yes, because she has been engaged to wait.
    b. Yes, because she is waiting to be engaged.
    c. No, because she has been engaged to wait.
    d. No, because she is waiting to be engaged.

79. How old must one be to take a job that has been designated hazardous by the Secretary of Labor?

    a. 16
    b. 18
    c. 21
    d. There is no age restriction on hazardous employment.

80. What is the distinguishing characteristic of a seamless organization?

    a. Low turnover
    b. Multiple chief executives
    c. Lack of hierarchy
    d. Employees report to two managers

81. Which of the following is NOT an injury or illness prevention plan required by OSHA?

    a. emergency action plan
    b. safety and health management plan
    c. sanitation plan
    d. fire prevention plan

82. The Green Company is putting together a group incentive. To begin with, management assesses the baseline productivity levels of the organization. Incentives are given when the group exceeds baseline productivity. What type of program has the Green Company established?

    a. gainsharing
    b. Scanlon Plan
    c. improshare
    d. profit sharing

83. Which of the following is a common problem during the growth phase of the organizational life cycle?

    a. outsourcing
    b. poor communication between management and employees
    c. excessive bureaucracy
    d. slow response to market changes

84. Which of the following is the least common reason for employees stationed in a foreign country to request a transfer back home?

    a. Local epidemics
    b. Culture shock
    c. Employee is homesick
    d. Employee's spouse or child is homesick

85. Which piece of federal legislation established that the United States will give preferential treatment to prospective immigrants who have special skills?

    a. Immigration Reform and Control Act of 1986
    b. Immigration Act of 1990
    c. Equal Employment Opportunity Act of 1972
    d. 1965 amendments to the Immigration and Nationality Act of 1952

86. Which of the following is a strategic function of the human resources department?

    a. Creating retention plans
    b. Recruiting new employees
    c. Ensuring compliance with federal regulations
    d. Keeping employee data confidential

87. In the United States, there is an expectation that employees will meet a minimum standard of effort and competence in their work. This is known as

    a. due process
    b. a mandatory minimum.
    c. the duty of diligence.
    d. the duty of loyalty.

88. How is gross profit calculated?

    a. The cost of goods sold is subtracted from total sales revenue.
    b. Operating expenses are subtracted from total profit.
    c. Liabilities are subtracted from the total value of the business.
    d. Distributions to owners are subtracted from net profits.

89. What piece of legislation led to the creation of generally accepted accounting principles (GAAP)?

    a. Omnibus Budget Reconciliation Act
    b. Norris-La Guardia Act
    c. Securities Exchange Act of 1934
    d. Sarbanes-Oxley Act

90. Which of the following statements about Six Sigma is false?

    a. Master black belts usually concentrate on quality in a single department.
    b. Defects are measured on a per-million basis.
    c. Green belts work full-time on quality management.
    d. The five-step method of Six Sigma is define, measure, analyze, improve, and control.

91. Sandra is the head of a small human resources department. She wants to implement a human resource information system, so she begins by commissioning a needs analysis. What is her next step?

    a. Researching possible systems
    b. Asking for permission to implement the system
    c. Identifying possible conflicts with other organizational systems
    d. Creating a timeline for implementation

92. How is the lost time rate calculated?

    a. Number of lost days per hundred employees divided by total number of employees, then multiplied by 100

    b. Number of lost time accidents divided by 200,000

    c. Number of OSHA recordables divided by 200,000

    d. Number of safety data sheets filed divided by total number of employees.

93. The Age Discrimination in Employment Act requires that any employee records related to charges of discrimination must be retained

    a. until the charges are resolved.

    b. for one year.

    c. for two years or until the charges are resolved, whichever comes first.

    d. for seven years.

94. Byron wants to analyze the relationship between the size of the holiday advertising budget and sales. Which analytical strategy will he use?

    a. trend analysis

    b. ratio

    c. simple linear regression

    d. multiple linear regression

95. What was the primary result of *Faragher v. City of Boca Raton* (1998)?

    a. Employers are not responsible for their employees' behavior.

    b. An adverse TEA need only be implied for harassment to be actionable.

    c. Sexual harassment that creates a hostile work environment is covered by Title VII.

    d. A work environment is considered hostile if it causes observable psychological injury.

96. How does the Family and Medical Leave Act define a "key employee"?

    a. Any employee who has subordinates

    b. Any employee whose skills cannot be easily replaced

    c. Any manager or executive

    d. Any employee whose salary is in the top 10% at the company

97. Which element of worker's compensation common law prevented employees from being compensated when their injury was caused by a colleague?

    a. doctrine of contributory negligence

    b. voluntary assumption of risk

    c. fellow servant rule

    d. good Samaritan law.

98. Barbara contracts the flu from her daughter. While she is at work, her stomach becomes upset and she vomits. She has to go home for the day. Is this a work-related illness?

    a. No, because vomiting is not considered a significant symptom.

    b. No, because the influenza exposure occurred away from work.

    c. Yes, because the symptoms were exhibited at work.

    d. Yes, because any incidents of vomiting must be reported.

99. According to the Pregnancy Discrimination Act of 1978, employers should treat pregnancy like a

   a. work-related illness.
   b. work-related injury.
   c. short-term disability.
   d. long-term disability.

100. One of the main purposes of the Foreign Corrupt Practices Act is to prohibit American businesses from doing what?

   a. Taking unfair advantage of foreign exchange rates
   b. Paying foreign nationals less than expatriates
   c. Making accommodations for sharia law in the workplace
   d. Paying bribes to foreign officials for favors or access

101. In which case was it determined that employees may not waive Family and Medical Leave Act (FMLA) rights in a severance agreement?

   a. Taylor v. Progress Energy, Inc. (2007)
   b. Phason v. Meridian Rail Corporation (2007)
   c. Smith v. City of Jackson, Mississippi (2005)
   d. Circuit *City Stores v. Adams* (2001)

102. A realistic job preview (RJP) should be used when

   a. unemployment is high.
   b. recruits have access to plenty of information about the job.
   c. the selection ratio is high.
   d. employee replacement costs are high.

103. Which piece of federal legislation created 401(k) plans for employees?

   a. Retirement Equity Act of 1984
   b. Tax Reform Act of 1986
   c. Revenue Act of 1978
   d. Employee Retirement Income Security Act of 1974

104. A small landscaping company argues that complying with ADA regulations would constitute an undue hardship. Which of the following company characteristics would NOT be considered by the government when evaluating this claim?

   a. Size of the company
   b. Location of the company
   c. Cost of making reasonable accommodations
   d. Financial status of the company

105. Nine weeks after giving birth, Deirdre comes back to work on a reduced schedule. Instead of her normal 40-hour week, she only works 30 hours. How many weeks of FMLA leave does Deirdre use for each of these thirty-hour weeks?

   a. 1/4
   b. 1/2
   c. 1
   d. 10

106. The United States Patent Act recognizes each of the following patent types except

    a. design patents.
    b. structure patents.
    c. plant patents.
    d. utility patents.

107. Derek is delivering a presentation to a group of trainees. During the presentation, the trainees will need to take comprehensive notes. How should Derek arrange the seats in the training room?

    a. conference style
    b. U-shaped style
    c. classroom style
    d. Chevron style

108. Which of the following is a passive method of training?

    a. case study
    b. vestibule
    c. presentation
    d. seminar

109. How many months of COBRA coverage do employees terminated for gross misconduct receive?

    a. None
    b. Six
    c. Twelve
    d. Eighteen

110. Which case determined that compensating employees for participation in work committees is not a violation of the National Labor Relations Act?

    a. *E.I.* DuPont & Co. v. NLRB (1993)
    b. McKennon v. Nashville Banner Publishing Company (1995)
    c. Johnson v. Santa Clara County Transportation Agency (1987)
    d. Electromation, *Inc. v. NLRB* (1992)

111. Which of the following is NOT one of the quality management phases identified by Joseph M. Juran?

    a. quality control
    b. quality planning
    c. quality selection
    d. quality improvement

112. Which compensation system is typical of unionized workplaces?

    a. seniority-based
    b. membership-based
    c. performance-based
    d. incentive-based

113. The FrogTech Company is growing rapidly, and needs to hire several new engineers. However, the candidates for these jobs are in high demand, so FrogTech has to increase the normal entry-level salary. The human resources department notes that new engineers at FrogTech will now be making almost the same salary as those who have been around for years. This scenario is known as

    a. pay differential.
    b. salary acceleration.
    c. wage garnishment.
    d. wage compression.

114. The final step in a job pricing exercise is

    a. a salary range recommendation.
    b. a wage target.
    c. hiring the least costly candidate.
    d. weighing candidate qualifications against available funds.

115. An employer believes that an employee has concealed a USB drive with valuable trade secrets on his person. Is the employer allowed to search the employee's body?

    a. Yes, but the search must be conducted by an employee of the same sex.
    b. Yes, but the search must be conducted by a law enforcement officer.
    c. No, because the employee has a reasonable expectation of privacy.
    d. No, because physical searches in the workplace are prohibited by law.

116. Which of these is NOT a benefit of the geocentric approach to international staffing?

    a. Easier communications with the home office
    b. Easier monitoring of standards compliance by the home office
    c. Goodwill from local citizens and authorities
    d. Employees are known quantities

117. Which metric compares the number of new employees to the total number of employees?

    a. replacement rate
    b. turnover rate
    c. accession rate
    d. succession rate

118. What was the founding idea of quality improvement, as espoused by W. Edwards Deming?

    a. The customer is the ultimate judge of quality.
    b. Defects can be reduced infinitely.
    c. Design is more important than function.
    d. Employees should continuously improve.

119. Which of the following is a rating method of performance appraisal?

    a. checklist
    b. field appraisal
    c. essay
    d. critical incident review

120. Which three factors does the HAY system use to classify jobs?

    a. knowledge, experience, and seniority
    b. knowledge, skill, and ability
    c. knowledge, accountability, and problem solving
    d. knowledge, skill, and responsibility

121. Which of the following is a primary reason for the failure of total quality management programs?

    a. Micromanaging by employees at all levels of the organizational hierarchy
    b. Overemphasis on core objectives
    c. Failure to use ISO 9000 standards
    d. Inability to identify the advantages of change

122. What are on the axes of the Blake-Mouton managerial grid?

    a. people and production
    b. profit and production
    c. people and profit
    d. people and presentation

123. Which method of reporting does the Department of Labor prefer with regard to time worked by employees who are nonexempt under the Fair Labor Standards Act?

    a. exception reporting
    b. selected reporting
    c. positive time reporting
    d. negative time reporting

124. After a corporation is taken over in a friendly acquisition, several executives are offered substantially higher compensation packages by the new company. What is the term that describes this kind of compensation package?

    a. Golden parachute
    b. Golden handshake
    c. Golden handcuffs
    d. Golden life jacket

125. Which piece of legislation made it illegal to discriminate on the basis of health?

    a. Retirement Equity Act of 1984
    b. Health Insurance Portability and Accountability Act of 1996
    c. Civil Rights Act of 1991
    d. Pregnancy Discrimination Act of 1978

126. Which of the following would be considered primary research?

    a. interviews performed by the researcher
    b. journal articles
    c. books
    d. trend analyses

127. Phil claims that he was not allowed to apply for an available position because of a standard defined as unlawful by the Americans with Disabilities Act. The hiring company claims that Phil was not qualified for the job in the first place. Which case is most relevant to Phil's situation?

    a. Sista v. CDC Ixis North America, Inc. (2006)
    b. Phason v. Meridian Rail Corporation (2007)
    c. Bates v. United Parcel Service (2006)
    d. Pharakhone *v. Nissan North America, Inc.* (2003)

128. How many managers does each employee report to in a matrix organization?

    a. 0
    b. 1
    c. 2
    d. 4

129. When Jared takes over a supervisory position in the marketing department, he tries to set a good example for his subordinates. He recognizes that there are already strong creative partnerships within the department, so he tries to foster even more cooperation. What style of leadership is Jared practicing?

    a. authoritarian leadership
    b. coaching
    c. democratic leadership
    d. transformational leadership

130. As part of his new job in the finance department, Julian is taught to use a new accounting program. However, he finds that he does not often need to use this program in his work. So, although he quickly attains decent competence with the program, he does not make much progress thereafter. Which style of learning curve illustrates this situation?

    a. plateau learning curve
    b. positively accelerating learning curve
    c. negatively accelerating learning curve
    d. S-shaped learning curve

131. During the opening conference of an OSHA inspection, the Compliance Health and Safety Officer requests an employee to accompany her around the facilities. What happens if no one volunteers?

    a. The company will receive a written reprimand.
    b. The inspection cannot continue.
    c. The CSHO will interview employees about their working conditions.
    d. The company will be fined a maximum of $10,000.

132. In which of the following businesses is the research and development department likely to be distinct from the marketing department?

    a. fertilizer manufacturer
    b. toy manufacturer
    c. publisher
    d. clothing manufacturer

133. The ADDIE model outlines the components of

    a. leadership.
    b. employee recruiting.
    c. manufacturing.
    d. instructional design.

134. Which of the following compensation packages or elements is most likely to create an incentive for an executive to take actions that might have a negative impact on a company in the long term?

    a. LEAPS
    b. Quarterly bonuses based on share price
    c. Golden parachute
    d. Defined contribution pension

135. As he arrives at work, Sven bumps into a tree in the company parking lot. He experiences some neck pain later in the day. Is this a work-related injury?

    a. No, injuries sustained in vehicle accidents on company property before or after work are not considered work-related.
    b. No, because Sven had not yet clocked in.
    c. Yes, because the accident took place on company property.
    d. Yes, because the symptoms emerged at work.

136. Which of the following is a provision of the Fair Labor Standards Act of 1938?

    a. All previous compensation laws are obsolete.
    b. Overtime pay must be 1.5 times the normal hourly wage.
    c. The maximum work week is 45 hours.
    d. Children may work unlimited hours, provided working conditions are safe.

137. When the federal and state minimum wages are different, which one takes precedence?

    a. State minimum wage
    b. Federal minimum wage
    c. The higher wage
    d. The lower wage

138. An executive develops a presentation in which he uses *Macbeth* to illustrate the perils and possibilities of ambition. Does the executive need to pay for the right to reference this work?

    a. No, this work is in the public domain.
    b. No, this falls under the fair use doctrine.
    c. Yes, this work is not in the public domain.
    d. Yes, this work does not fall under the fair use doctrine.

139. What are the four Ps of marketing?

    a. product, price, payment, persistence
    b. preview, position, price, persuasion
    c. product, price, place, promotion
    d. promotion, place, position, (market) penetration

140. In which case did the Supreme Court rule that job requirements must be demonstrably related to the job?

a. Automobile Workers v. Johnson Controls (1977)
b. Griggs v. Duke Power (1971)
c. Albemarle Paper v. Moody (1975)
d. NLRB *v. J. Weingarten, Inc.* (1975)

141. Why might a company's total rewards packages lag the market?

a. The company is trying to attract top talent.
b. The company is trying to establish itself in a new area.
c. Turnover is high at the company.
d. The company's sales have increased sharply.

142. The Youngblood Company is too small to have its own health insurance plan, so it joins several other businesses in a combined plan. This is known as a(n)

a. administrative services only plan.
b. third party administrator plan.
c. partially self-funded plan.
d. health purchasing alliance.

143. The Greendale Company is thinking about adjusting its executive compensation package. There is some concern, however, that the new program will adversely affect the company's tax burden. The Greendale Company should ask the IRS for a(n)

a. trade exception.
b. audit.
c. private letter ruling.
d. expansion clause.

144. Phyllis wants to hire several college students as seasonal employees in her shop. She refers to these students to a temp agency, who hires them and sends them to work for Phyllis. This is called

a. payrolling.
b. on-call employment.
c. in-house employment.
d. temp-to-perm employment.

145. Summarize the ruling in Taxman v. Board of Education of Piscataway (1993).

a. Employees on FMLA leave may be fired if they break the rules of the company.
b. Protected classes may not be given preferential treatment during layoffs if they have not been discriminated against or underrepresented before.
c. Sexual orientation is a protected class.
d. Employers are vicariously liable for supervisor harassment of employees.

146. Hubert contracts food poisoning from a tuna fish sandwich he made at home. He eats the sandwich in the break room and becomes sick in the employee bathroom. Is this a work-related illness?

a. Yes, because the food was consumed at the workplace.
b. Yes, because he became sick at the workplace.
c. No, because food poisoning is not a significant illness.
d. No, because the food was prepared at home for personal consumption.

147. In Vroom's expectancy theory, what is the name for the reasoned decision to work?

    a. valence
    b. instrumentality
    c. proclivity
    d. expectancy

148. Which of the following statements about payroll systems is false?

    a. Payroll systems must monitor tax payments.
    b. Large companies often develop their own payroll software.
    c. Payroll systems must maintain employee confidentiality.
    d. Payroll systems are always the responsibility of the human resources department.

149. The Uniform Guidelines on Employee Selection Procedures declare that

    a. employers may never use selection tools that adversely impact protected classes.
    b. employers may use whichever selection tool they prefer.
    c. employers must use the selection tool that has the least adverse impact on protected classes.
    d. a selection tool has an adverse impact when the hiring rate for protected classes is less than half the rate for the class hired most often.

150. Which of the following statements about unions is true?

    a. Unions may require employers to terminate anti-union employees.
    b. Unions may not be held liable for coercive acts by union members.
    c. Unions may not participate in secondary boycotts.
    d. Unions may picket even where another union is the legal bargaining representative.

151. According to Feldman's model of organizational socialization, in which stage do new employees confirm or dismiss the expectations held before hiring?

    a. change
    b. encounter
    c. anticipatory socialization
    d. acquisition

152. Which of these businesses is most likely to have an outbreak of tuberculosis?

    a. assisted-living facility
    b. day care center
    c. restaurant
    d. gas station

153. How are immigrant visas allocated by the United States government?

    a. first come, first served
    b. according to nationality
    c. according to the number of family members who are US citizens
    d. according to work experience

154. Which of the following is NOT a source of motivation identified in McClelland's acquired needs theory?

 a. achievement
 b. power
 c. affiliation
 d. wealth

155. In the view of the Office of Federal Contract Compliance Programs, what is the best source for data related to employee race and ethnicity?

 a. self-reporting
 b. census forms
 c. birth certificates
 d. employer judgment

156. In a collective bargaining agreement, which clause requires all new employees to join the union within a defined interval?

 a. maintenance of membership clause
 b. closed shop clause
 c. union shop clause
 d. contract administration clause

157. Which of the following would reduce information overload during orientation?

 a. Focus on the positive aspects of the organization
 b. Handing out documents supplementary to lecture material
 c. Conducting the program in one installment rather than in a series of meetings
 d. Preventing open-ended discussion after presentations

158. Which word best characterizes employee movement in the team-based model of career development?

 a. lateral
 b. upward
 c. static
 d. frequent

159. An American citizen is transferred abroad. Her annual salary is $300,000 US. She returns to the US for visits with friends and family for three weeks each year; she spends the rest of the year in the foreign country. Using 2014 figures, how much of her annual salary is exempt from US income taxes?

 a. approximately $199,000
 b. approximately $99,000
 c. approximately $59,000
 d. approximately $159,000

160. Which of the following is a consequence of the Sarbanes-Oxley Act?

 a. Employees may trade stock during pension fund blackout periods.
 b. Companies are allowed to conduct their own stock appraisal.
 c. CEOs may be punished for fraudulent financial reports.
 d. Audit partners must alternate every two years.

161. Employee morale is likely to suffer the most in the run-up to which of the following events:

    a. The company being merged with another in a hostile takeover
    b. The company being merged with another in a friendly acquisition
    c. The company selling off one of its divisions
    d. The company using a hostile takeover to acquire another company

162. Which of the following is NOT an essential component of an intellectual property agreement?

    a. Identification of confidential information
    b. Prohibition against the hiring of current employees by employees who leave the business
    c. Limitations on use of confidential information
    d. Duration of confidentiality restrictions

163. Which of the following is considered indirect compensation?

    a. variable compensation
    b. performance bonus
    c. leave of absence
    d. base pay

164. Your company is merging with Acme Enterprises in a friendly acquisition. Which of these employee documents or records would you NOT request from Acme?

    a. Names and addresses
    b. Contracts of employment
    c. Citizenship status
    d. Marital status

165. Identify the components of the four-dimensional model of management.

    a. audience, employees, responsibilities, actions
    b. recruitment, performance, transition, responsibility
    c. functions, roles, targets, styles
    d. leadership, subordination, administration, facilitation

166. Which of the following is a voluntary deduction from gross earnings?

    a. Social Security
    b. state income tax
    c. Medicare
    d. 401(k) contribution

167. In which type of dispute resolution do both parties agree to accept whatever decision is reached by the third party judge?

    a. binding arbitration
    b. compulsory arbitration
    c. constructive confrontation
    d. ad hoc arbitration

168. When one company acquires another, what is the first step for the acquiring company's human resources department?

    a. Survey of the workforce for both organizations
    b. Elimination of redundant positions
    c. Review of collective bargaining agreements
    d. Assurance of OSHA compliance

169. Who should conduct exit interviews?

    a. human resources officers
    b. senior executives
    c. a third party
    d. departmental managers

170. The extent to which the results of research can accurately identify a difference between trained and untrained employees is called

    a. statistical significance.
    b. marginal difference.
    c. selectivity.
    d. statistical power.

171. For their first few months, new employees at Flanders Company receive frequent praise and encouragement from their supervisors. After a while, though, supervisors pay less attention to these employees. Performance evaluations indicate that employee productivity declines at this point. The supervisors at Flanders Company are practicing

    a. punishment.
    b. positive reinforcement.
    c. negative reinforcement.
    d. extinction.

172. A corporate university is an

    a. academic institution run for profit.
    b. independent academic institution that produces recruits for a corporation.
    c. extensive training program administered by a corporation to existing employees.
    d. alternative to community college.

173. In the sales department of Fitch Company, employees know that the size of their annual bonus is tied to their performance. The company has published a chart indicating the relationship between sales and compensation. The employees of Fitch Company have

    a. an entitlement philosophy.
    b. line of sight.
    c. intrinsic rewards.
    d. fiduciary responsibility.

174. The Davis-Bacon Act is notable for being the first federal legislation to address

    a. government subcontractors.
    b. minimum wages.
    c. overtime compensation.
    d. child labor.

175. What are the four styles of leadership identified by the Hersey-Blanchard theory?

    a. telling, selling, participating, delegating
    b. showing, growing, sowing, bestowing
    c. managing, administrating, inspiring, following
    d. giving, taking, making, doing

Answer Key and Explanations

1. C: Bachelor's degree. A foreigner needs to have the equivalent of a four-year college degree in order to qualify for the H-1B visa program. This program allows people to come to America on a temporary basis to work in occupations in fields such as math, engineering, architecture, physical science, biotechnology, social science, medicine/health, and law.

2. A: In a limited liability partnership, partners exist mainly as investors, without much influence on daily operations. This arrangement, which is also known simply as a limited partnership, is typical of professional businesses, like legal or accounting firms. A sole proprietorship is initiated and operated by a single person. This person is entitled to all of the profits, but is liable for all business activities. In a general partnership, the business operates according to a preset agreement, and liability is shared by a group of partners. The joint venture is a form of general partnership created for a particular purpose or a restricted amount of time.

3. B: The Civil Rights Act of 1991 declared that back pay awards cannot be a part of compensatory damages. This act also made it illegal for businesses to claim that discriminatory practices were somehow necessary to their operations. This act also directly prohibited all racial harassment, whereas earlier legislation had limited its scope to hiring practices.

4. D: The SMART model outlines the important characteristics of corporate goals. This model asserts that goals should be specific, measurable, action-based, realistic, and time-based. In other words, they should be detailed, capable of assessment, based on concrete activities, attainable, and scheduled.

5. C: One consequence of the Clayton Act of 1914 was that employers could not use injunctions to break strikes. This act was intended to protect the free market from monopolies and exclusive business arrangements. This act was unique at the time because it made executives responsible for violations.

6. A: Ranking is not a good method for appraising large groups of employees. The ranking method simply entails placing jobs in order from most important to least. In a large organization, it will be difficult to make comparisons between jobs. Also, many job groups will be so different that comparisons will be worthless. The other answer choices are true statements. In a forced ranking system, the appraisers place all employees on a bell curve, and therefore the vast majority end up close to the middle.

7. A: Flex time is considered nonmonetary compensation. Non-monetary compensation is any reward that is not money or that cannot be monetized. The other answer choices represent compensation that is an expense for the business. Flex time systems allow employees to work variable hours of the day, which can be very useful for employees who have numerous responsibilities outside of work.

8. C: The Small Business Job Protection Act of 1996 established a new definition for "highly compensated individual." This act also created a new retirement plan for small businesses and altered the rules regarding S corporations.

9. D: In business, the primary difference between a goal and a strategy is that a strategy is a means, while a goal is an end. Businesses create strategies for reaching their goals. The achievements that must be made on the way to the accomplishment of the goal are known as objectives. Goals are more general and long-term objectives.

10. B: The situation outlined above can be defined as role conflict. Role conflict exists when an employee does not understand exactly what is expected of him. This problem is common when an employee must report to more than one superior. Role orientation is the process of becoming familiar with an employee role. Role overload is a sense of anxiety or panic produced by a perception that one is being asked to do too much. Role ambiguity is a general lack of clarity regarding the parameters of the employee role. Goal ambiguity is particularly common when a new position has been created within the organization, and the requirements of the position have yet to be finalized.

11. A: The Equal Employment Opportunity Act of 1972 did not extend Title VII coverage to the employees of religious institutions. These organizations were exempted from the original version of Title VII (in the Civil Rights Act of 1964), and this exemption was maintained in 1972. Religious institutions are allowed to give preferential treatment to job candidates and employees who are adherents of that religion. Universities, state government agencies, and federal legislative bodies all became subject to Title VII with the passage of the Equal Employment Opportunity Act.

12. B: A pesticide is an example of a chemical health hazard. The other three answer choices are biological health hazards. OSHA requires businesses to maintain safety data sheets related to every chemical found in the workplace. A safety data sheet outlines the components of the substance, as well as its behavior under various conditions. Most importantly, the safety data sheet indicates whether a chemical is harmful when absorbed, inhaled, or ingested, and how these dangers may be mitigated or avoided.

13. C: This is an example of risk mitigation. The Stanley Corporation minimizes the potential for lawsuits by monitoring its own compliance. Some risks cannot be entirely avoided; there is no perfect strategy for avoiding litigation. This risk cannot be eliminated. Risk transfer is similar to risk mitigation, but it involves increasing expense in one area to minimize a risk elsewhere. For instance, a company might increase insurance payments to account for a particular risk.

14. D: The Workforce Investment Act led to the creation of comprehensive training centers for workers and employers. The intention of this act was to decrease welfare rolls and improve productivity. The training centers created pursuant to this act offer a broad range of support for workers and employers alike.

15. D: According to Edward E. Lawler, the four elements of a high-involvement organization are power, information, knowledge and rewards. A high-involvement organization is one in which employees are given the opportunity to arrange their work schedules and processes. In other words, employees have the power to determine their own day-to-day activities. Of course, they are also responsible for results. In Lawler's system, a high-involvement organization makes a wealth of information available to all employees, so that it can factor into their decision-making process. Similarly, a high-involvement organization continuously tries to improve the employee knowledge base. Finally, in a high-involvement organization, employees are paid based on their performance rather than seniority.

16. A: Decertification does not prevent employees from joining a different union later. Indeed, decertification does not prevent employees from rejoining the same union in the future. Decertification is not always indicative of problems with the union. In some cases, a union will decertify because it has outgrown its usefulness, or because the workers wish to file suit against ownership without the interference of the union. Employers are not allowed to lobby employees during the decertification process, and only 30% of the employees need to petition the NLRB for there to be a decertification vote.

17. C: In *Weeks v. Southern Bell Telephone Company* (1969), the Fifth Circuit determined that a company may not claim physical difficulty as a bona fide occupational qualification in order to keep women out of certain jobs. This case centered on a woman who was denied an available position within the company because it entailed some heavy lifting. She asserted that this was discrimination. The company admitted prima facie discrimination but argued unsuccessfully that the ability to lift heavy objects was a bona fide occupational qualification.

18. B: In an affirmative action plan, the determination of availability provides demographic information for the labor market related to each job group. Specifically, this part of the affirmative action plan indicates how many women and minorities are available to fill positions in each job group. A determination of availability should include internal and external candidates. A job group analysis indicates how the business categorizes various positions. The comparison of incumbency to availability calculates the company's success at employing minorities compared with the job market as a whole. Finally, the organizational profile is a simple list of the positions within the business.

19. D: One common problem with cost-per-hire metrics is that they omit costs that are not related to specific candidates. The cost-per-hire measure is determined by dividing total costs by number of hires. It is important that the costs and hires be taken from the same time interval. To be comprehensive, a cost-per-hire measure should include the salaries of those employed to make hires, the cost of advertising, and any other administrative costs incurred during the hiring process.

20. A: The new employee can expect to work in a small group during the training session. In banquet-style seating, participants are placed in small groups around several tables. They will be able to turn and face a single presenter if necessary, but they will probably be spending most of their time interacting with their tablemates.

21. C: Ron and Marcy have participated in patterned interviews. This type of interview covers a predetermined set of subjects, but does not adhere to a script. In other words, the interviewer will know in advance what topics are to be discussed, but will not have a list of questions to be asked verbatim. Patterned interviews allow the interviewer to follow up on interesting and provocative comments, but the resulting interviews may be difficult to compare. A structured interview follows a predetermined list of questions. In a stress interview, the prospective employee is subjected to a very difficult or challenging situation. A non-directive interview is a free-form conversation that may range over any number of topics.

22. C: Employees may not strike to support a hot cargo clause. A cargo clause is a pledge made by the employer to the union that the employer will not enter into transactions with some other employer. The other answer choices are true statements.

23. D: Company X is using a divestiture people processing strategy. This type of strategy aims to reduce the influence of personal characteristics on the organization. Military institutions typically employ a divestiture people processing strategy, with the aim of making individual soldiers subservient to the imperatives of the group. Investiture people processing strategies, on the other hand, give new employees a chance to express themselves and apply their personal idiosyncrasies to the organization. Contest people processing strategies do not sort new employees by interest or ability; instead, they put every new employee through the same program, and make decisions about placement once orientation is complete. Finally, collective people processing strategies emphasize cooperation between new employees.

- 29 -

24. B: The Norris-LaGuardia Act of 1932 forbade yellow dog contracts, in which employees promise not to join a union. This law also made it more difficult for the courts to issue injunctions that would stop a strike. The act was seen as a victory for workers.

25. A: A correlation coefficient of +0.8 would be the strongest suggestion that productivity increases with experience. Only a positive correlation coefficient indicates that productivity and experience are positively correlated. A negative correlation coefficient would indicate that productivity declines with experience. For this reason, the answer is +0.8, even though -0.9 (answer choice D) represents the strongest correlation.

26. C: Businesses can decide to test certain job groups only. Some businesses restrict their drug testing to employees who will have great responsibility or who will be operating heavy machinery. Scheduled drug testing programs are less effective, because drug-using employees are given a chance to devise ways around the test. Businesses may test only some candidates, though they must be consistent with respect to the tested job groups.

27. D: In *Regents of California v. Bakke* (1978), the Supreme Court ruled that universities may not use quotas to boost minority admissions. This case centered on a white man who was denied admission to medical school twice, though in both years minority students with lower grades and test scores were admitted. The white man, Allan Bakke, claimed reverse discrimination. The Supreme Court declared that it was unconstitutional for the University of California to base minority admissions on a quota, though race could be a factor in admissions decisions.

28. C: In zero-based budgeting, every expense must be justified. Zero-based budgeting programs attempt to streamline the business by judging the necessity of every item. Historical budgeting, on the other hand, assumes that the expenses from previous years will be carried over. Obviously, zero-based budgeting is a more time-consuming process, though it can produce substantial savings. Zero-based and historical budgeting programs may be executed in a top-down or bottom-up fashion, depending on whether top managers or all relevant managers are included.

29. A: An employee's performance on an assembly line is likely to follow a negatively accelerating learning curve. This type of learning curve is typical of rote tasks, which can be learned and indeed mastered in a short time, but which do not permit much improvement after the initial learning. A positively accelerating learning curve, on the other hand, is marked by a slow start followed by a gradually increasing speed of learning. A positively accelerating learning curve is typical of complex tasks, which are difficult at first but which may be improved upon over a long interval.

30. B: The Americans with Disabilities Act does not count driving as a major life activity. According to the act, major life activities are personal care, manual tasks, seeing, hearing, eating, sleeping, breathing, learning, reading, concentrating, thinking, communicating, and working. However, a person may also be covered by the ADA when certain physical or mental impairments are present, including "any physiological disorder or condition, cosmetic disfigurement, or anatomical loss affecting one or more body systems, such as neurological, musculoskeletal, special sense organs, respiratory (including speech organs), cardiovascular, reproductive, digestive, genitourinary, immune, circulatory, hemic, lymphatic, skin, and endocrine; or ... any mental or psychological disorder, such as an intellectual disability ... organic brain syndrome, emotional or mental illness, and specific learning disabilities." (Code of Federal Regulations, 29CFR1630)

31. C: One possible drawback of this arrangement is a lack of communication among the foreign offices. The Archibald Corporation is using what is known as the polycentric approach to international staffing. The advantages to this system are that it is cheaper to employ foreign

nationals than to use expatriates and that it gives the foreign community a sense of investment in the business. However, if a corporation has multiple overseas offices, linguistic and cultural barriers may impede communication among them.

32. B: The Family Medical Leave Act of 1993 requires employers to give new mothers at least twelve weeks of unpaid leave. New mothers and fathers can take this leave once in a twelve-month period. Employees are required to give thirty days' notice before taking FMLA leave. Also, in order to take this leave an employee must have been working for the company for at least a year, or 1250 hours.

33. B: A physician hospital organization makes contract arrangements directly with employers. In this system, physicians and hospitals act as a single entity. In a health maintenance organization (HMO), patients are managed by a gatekeeper physician, who refers them to other medical professionals when necessary. In a preferred provider organization, patients work with a designated network of medical professionals. Fee-for-service plans allow the patient to shop around for medical services, the costs of which are initially covered by the patient, who is later reimbursed.

34. C: Since the Williamson Company is using the paired comparison method, each member of the sales job group will be compared with six other people. The paired comparison method requires every member of the job group to be compared to every other member. This means that each member of the Williamson Company's sales group will be compared to the other six members. The paired comparison method is a good way to rank employees systematically.

35. D: Philip B. Crosby's four absolutes of quality are conformance to requirements, prevention, performance standards, and measurement. Crosby considered effective management the most important determinant of quality. In his view, the first criterion of quality was the extent to which products and processes conform to the standards set by management. *Prevention* refers to intentional efforts to avoid mistakes. *Performance standards* refers to establishing high expectations. *Measurement* refers to a comprehensive program for assessing employee performance.

36. D: In Alderfer's theory of motivation, the letters ERG stand for existence, relatedness, and growth. Like Maslow, Alderfer asserted that basic needs must be met before a person can attend to more sophisticated desires. Whereas Maslow defined the hierarchy of needs, in ascending levels of importance, as physiological, safety, love, status, and esteem, Alderfer reduced it to three. The first, existence, refers to all the activities aimed at maintaining life. The second, relatedness, refers to the need for connection with other people. The third, growth, is the innate human desire for personal evolution.

37. C: In *School Board of Nassau v. Arline*, the Supreme Court ruled that contagious diseases should be treated as handicaps under Section 504 of the Rehabilitation Act. This case was based on a schoolteacher who had tuberculosis and was unable to work for a long while, during which time she was fired. The Supreme Court ruled that employers are responsible for making reasonable accommodations for employees with contagious diseases.

38. B: A Pareto chart indicates the changes that will produce the greatest improvement. This chart looks like a combination of a bar graph and a line graph. The bars indicate the various causes of a particular problem, while the line indicates the improvement that would result from eliminating each of these causes. This chart is based on the Pareto principle, which is that 80% of the inefficiencies in a process can be removed by changing only 20% of the causes. In other words, a

few causes have outsized influence on the process. A histogram, on the other hand, is used to identify patterns in seemingly random events. A stratification chart breaks a complex problem down into its constituent elements. An Ishikawa diagram, otherwise known as a cause-and-effect diagram, illustrates all of the steps in a process, with the aim of identifying redundancies and inefficiencies.

39. B: A short-form employment application would be the most appropriate in this situation. The Henderson Company is hiring for an unskilled position, so it should not have extensive requirements for candidates. Using a short-form employment application will minimize the amount of reading for the human resources department. Longer applications should only be used when necessary.

40. A: This labor union is using a parallel bargaining strategy. Parallel bargaining is often used when the union believes that one particular employer will agree to an especially favorable deal. By negotiating this deal first, the union can set a standard that other employers will reluctantly meet. In the integrative bargaining approach, the union and employers lay all the facts on the table and compromise. In positional bargaining, the union and the employer are adversaries, each side using its leverage to get as much as possible. In multi-unit bargaining, a single employer must deal with multiple unions representing different job groups.

41. B: The tendency to overemphasize the impact of personality on behavior is known as the fundamental attribution error. The fundamental attribution error creates problems for organizations when managers punish poor performers rather than try to resolve the issues that are responsible for the poor performance.

42. D: The Personal Responsibility and Work Opportunity Reconciliation Act of 1996 governs Dennis' conduct in this situation. This act also ended the designation of welfare as an entitlement program and mandated that welfare recipients begin working after receiving benefits for two years.

43. D: Corporations fund business operations through the sale of stock. The purchasers of the stock are known as shareholders, and they are the ultimate owners of the corporation. They appoint a board of directors, which oversees the day-to-day managers of the corporation. When a corporation is successful, shareholders are paid dividends. When a corporation is unsuccessful, the value of stock shares may plummet.

44. A: *Payne v. The Western & Atlantic Railroad Company* (1884) first defined *employment at-will*. In this case, the Tennessee Supreme Court ruled that employment at-will is an arrangement that either side may terminate at any time. Of course, this definition led to many abuses by employers until subsequent legislation clarified the rights of workers.

45. B: The point factor method is used to identify the most important positions in an organization. In this method, organizational leaders assign a certain number of points to each organization depending on various factors, as for instance the responsibility, the education required, and the working conditions. The total number of points assigned to each job group indicates its significance to the organization.

46. C: Brian has a legitimate complaint because FMLA leave is to be treated the same as other forms of leave with regard to perfect attendance bonuses. Employers have the right to count FMLA leave against perfect attendance awards, but they must treat other forms of leave the same way. Since the employer did not count Jill's leave against her perfect attendance record, he may not count Brian's against him either. Alternatively, the employer could instead disqualify both Brian and Jill from the perfect attendance bonus.

47. C: ERISA (the Employee Retirement Income Security Act of 1974) mandates that employees who use graded vesting must be fully vested in a qualified plan within seven years. The original version of this act had looser vesting requirements. ERISA also asserts that employees who use cliff vesting must be fully vested in a qualified plan within five years.

48. C: The median bonus for salesmen at Franklin Company is $1000. The median is that number which evenly divides a set of numbers. In this case, there are five bonuses, and when arranged in order, the value $1000 lies at position 3, in the middle. The mean of a set of numbers is the same as the average. It is calculated by adding the numbers and dividing the sum by the total number of values in the set. So, in this case, the calculation is performed (500 + 750 + 1000 + 1000 + 1500) ÷ 5 = 950. The minimum value of a set is the lowest value, which is $500. Answer D represents the total, or sum, of the group of numbers.

49. B: A SWOT analysis would be most useful during the environmental scanning phase of the strategic planning process. During this phase, the strategy team tries to get the most accurate picture of the current state of the organization. A SWOT (strengths, weaknesses, opportunities, and threats) analysis is a common template for organizational self-assessment. It is a useful format because it requires planners to consider both internal (strengths and weaknesses) and external (opportunities and threats) factors.

50. A: A bank that issues United States savings bonds must complete an annual EEO (equal employment opportunity) survey. This form must be completed before September 30, and must use employment data from a pay period of the most recent July, August, or September. The point of this survey is to ensure that employers are not discriminating in their hiring or promotion practices. Institutions of higher education, state and local governments with more than 100 employees, and federal subcontractors with more than 100 employees are not required to file an EEO survey.

51. C: The national lost work day index (LWDI) average for private-sector organizations is approximately 2.5. This means that there are about 2.5 lost work days per day for every hundred employees. This figure is calculated by the Occupational Health and Safety Administration. LWDI is calculated by dividing the number of workdays missed because of personal injury for each hundred employees, dividing by the total number of employees, and then multiplying by a hundred.

52. D: Of the given correlation coefficients, -0.9 would indicate the strongest relationship between the two variables. Correlation coefficients exist on a range from -1 to +1. The strength of the correlation is indicated by the distance from zero, or absolute value, of the coefficient. In other words, whether a correlation coefficient is positive or negative does not influence its strength.

53. D: The Worker Adjustment and Retraining Notification Act stipulates that employers with more than a hundred employees must provide at least sixty days notice to workers and unions before closing a factory or plant. This legislation is generally referred to as the WARN Act. Its intention was not only to alert employees, but to enable the federal government to assist in the retraining of the soon-to-be-displaced workers.

54. A: Vince's compa-ratio is 80%. Compa-ratio is calculated by dividing the individual salary by the midpoint of the base salary for the job group, and then multiplying the quotient by 100. It is a handy way of comparing one person's salary with the salaries of other people who fill the same position.

55. D: In *Washington v. Davis* (1976), the Supreme Court ruled that employee selection tools predictive of success on the job are lawful even if they adversely impact a protected class. This case centered on two African-American prospective police officers who claimed an aptitude test administered during the application process discriminated against them. However, the Supreme

Court ruled that the aptitude test was a good predictor of success as a police officer, and was therefore lawful.

56. C: A Scanlon Plan is an example of a group incentive. When a business implements a Scanlon Plan, employees are given a share of whatever savings they can create for the company. In order for a Scanlon Plan to work, employees must have access to the company's financial data. This is considered a group incentive because it depends on the performance of the company as a whole and because the reward is given to each employee in the same measure.

57. A: For human resources departments, the first step in enterprise risk management is an audit. Enterprise risk management is a systematic assessment of the potential dangers to an organization, as well as the creation of a strategy to mitigate these dangers. A human resources audit looks for areas in which the business is at risk, whether because of suboptimal working conditions or noncompliance with regulations. Employee interviews may be a part of the audit. The purchase of insurance may be one consequence of an audit. Forecasting may only occur after the completion of an audit.

58. B: A high school janitor with the keys to the school generator would be most likely to receive on-call pay, compensation given to employees who must be available in case of emergency. Many doctors are on call, but they rarely receive special pay for this time, and dermatologists field few emergency requests. A receptionist would not need to be on call very often. A police officer is always on call, and does not receive special pay.

59. D: A wildcat strike is launched despite a no-strike clause in the employee contract. Obviously, these strikes create intense conflict between employer and union. Sit-down strikes, which are prohibited by law, occur inside the work facility. Secondary boycotts are attempts by the union to keep an external company from doing business with the employer. In most cases, secondary strikes are illegal. A hot cargo strike, more commonly known as a hot cargo picket, aims to keep the employer from doing business with some other employer opposed by the union. Hot cargo pickets are prohibited by law as well.

60. C: Yolanda will sign a third-party contract with the temp agency. A third-party contract requires actions to be taken by a party other than the two signing the deal. In this case, the temporary workers are addressed in the contract even though they do not sign it.

61. A: The Consumer Credit Protection Act of 1968 made it illegal to discharge an employee after only one garnishment order. This provision is to be enforced by the Wage and Hour Division of the Department of Labor. The section of the Consumer Credit Protection Act that deals with wage garnishment is Title III.

62. B: Fran's decision demonstrates the horn effect. This phenomenon, also known as the harshness bias, is the tendency to allow one irritating aspect of the interviewee's performance to dominate perception. An interviewer should be aware of this potential pitfall, and should consider whether the characteristic he finds distracting will likely be so to other people, or whether it bears significantly on job performance. In this case, Glenda's voice will probably not have much effect on her performance as an accountant. The central tendency, meanwhile, is a bias towards rating all candidates roughly equal. Stereotyping bias is a tendency to attribute certain characteristics to an interviewee because of his gender, ethnicity, religion, etc. The cultural noise bias is created when an interviewee answers questions not honestly, but in the way he believes the interviewer wants them to be answered.

63. B: Third-country nationals. Corporations with operations in foreign countries typically find themselves employing a wide variety of workers. Many are from the same country where the corporation is based. These employees are known as expatriates, or parent-country nationals. Others are from the country where the actual work is taking place; these are host-country nationals. Workers hailing from neither country are referred to as third-country nationals.

64. B: Pie charts are not commonly used in total quality management. Total quality management is a comprehensive approach to reducing errors and streamlining every aspect of an organization's operations. The other answer choices are charts frequently used to identify waste and make TQM plans. A Pareto chart combines line and bar graphs to identify the problems that are causing the most waste. A scatter plot represents the relationship between two variables. A histogram looks like a bar graph; it is used to identify variations in a set of experimental data.

65. A: A brown-bag lunch is an example of bottom-up communication. Bottom-up communication is directed from employees to managers. It is important for employees to have a chance to share their ideas and problems with more senior officials. A brown-bag lunch is an informal mealtime gathering of executives and lower-level employees. The other answer choices are forms of top-down communication, or communication directed from managers to lower-level employees.

66. D: Joint training programs are administered by unions and management. Their purpose is to maintain the skills and competence of union members. These programs are typically only available to members of the union. Most of these programs focus on safety or skills. Some unions have partnered with nearby academic institutions to deliver joint training programs.

67. B: The Delphi technique requires several rounds of questioning before a consensus is reached. In this method of decision-making, a panel of anonymous experts is given a short questionnaire. Their written responses are subjected to another series of questions. This process continues until a consensus is reached. The Delphi technique is good for getting a wide range of honest perspectives, and is convenient when the participants are geographically distant from one another.

68. C: According to conventional business wisdom, a mid-range plan can be executed in two years. The typical formulation is that short-range plans can be achieved in from six months to a year, midrange plans can be achieved in between one and three years, and long-range plans can be accomplished in three to five years. Most business experts assert that it is not worthwhile to plan much longer than five years in advance, because of the volatility and constant flux of the marketplace.

69. B: Steve has worked five hours of overtime. According to the Fair Labor Standards Act, paid holidays do not count as overtime. So, for the purpose of his overtime calculation, Steve has only worked 45 hours this week. Therefore, he has only worked five hours of overtime.

70. C: Fernando is owed reporting pay. He has been asked to come in at a certain time, so he should not be penalized or uncompensated simply because the boss has made an error. Typically, reporting pay is less than a full day's wage. On-call pay is given to employees who may be called in to deal with an emergency at any time. Not all employees who are on call are paid for it. Employees who are forced to return to work either before or after their allotted time may be eligible for call-back pay. Shift pay, finally, is the compensation associated with the employee's normal work schedule.

71. A: The primary directive of the Federal Employees Compensation Act of 1916 is to allocate funds to federal workers injured while performing their jobs. This was the first major piece of

workers' compensation legislation for federal employees. It asserted that federal workers' compensation cases were to be handled by the Department of Labor.

72. D: In this situation, the human resources officer should conduct a nondirective interview. Nondirective interviews follow no particular plan: they are more like casual conversations between the interviewer and the candidate. Because the available position remains undefined, it would not be fruitful to ask specific questions or to identify particular knowledge and skills. A non-directive interview would be a better way to determine whether candidates have the right attitude and temperament for the organization. Directive interviews follow a predetermined list of questions. A panel interview features multiple interviewers, typically from different departments. A stress interview requires the candidate to react to a demanding situation.

73. C: The Portal to Portal Act established that employees may not demand payment for their commute time. This act, which was passed in 1947, also required employers to pay for work performed before or after normal hours or during scheduled breaks.

74. C: The typical hours of the swing shift are 4 p.m. to 12 a.m. The day shift typically runs from 8 a.m. to 4 p.m., and the graveyard shift typically extends from 12 a.m. to 8 a.m. Some employees receive extra compensation for working the swing or graveyard shift.

75. D: Under the Civil Rights Act of 1991, the largest possible damage award is $300,000. Only businesses with more than 500 employees may be assessed this amount. Businesses with from 15 to 100 employees may be liable for damage awards of up to $50,000. Businesses with from 101 to 200 employees may be liable for damage awards of up to $100,000. Businesses with from 201 to 500 employees may be liable for damage awards of up to $200,000.

76. C: Context is not part of Kirkpatrick's training evaluation framework. Even though it was created in 1967, Kirkpatrick's description of training evaluation is still widely used. It outlines four criteria: reaction, learning, job behavior, and results. Reaction is the trainee's immediate response to the program. Learning is the information and skills that were obtained during the program. It is important that trainees acquire the skills they are supposed to acquire during training. Job behavior is the extent to which what has been learned during training is applied to real work. Finally, results are the overall impact of the training program on company performance.

77. D: Marsha has earned 45 hours of compensatory time off. Compensatory time off is calculated as 1.5 times the amount of overtime. Since Marsha worked 30 hours of overtime, her compensatory time off can be calculated by multiplying 30 by 1.5.

78. A: Tara should be compensated for this time, because she has been engaged to wait. She is not responsible for the flight delay, and so long as her employer wants her to keep waiting for the delayed flight, she should continue to be compensated.

79. B: A person must be at least 18 years old to take a job that has been designated hazardous by the Secretary of Labor. The Fair Labor Standards Act instituted a number of policies to prevent the exploitation of children. The only hazardous jobs children younger than 18 may be allowed to perform are related to farming.

80. C: The distinguishing characteristic of a seamless organization is a lack of hierarchy. In a seamless organization, employees are not placed in departments and restricted in their communication. The traditional boundaries within an organization, whether departmental or geographic, do not exist.

81. C: OSHA does not require businesses to create a sanitation plan, though the act does require businesses to meet certain standards in this regard. OSHA does require emergency action, safety and health management, and fire prevention plans. These plans must include a summation of company policy, the process for communicating this policy, record-keeping protocols, and identification of relevant officials.

82. C: The Green Company has established an improshare program. In this type of group incentive program, employees are rewarded for performing above a pre-established baseline standard. If the employees consistently exceed the baseline, it may be raised in the future. A gainsharing program is a more general attempt to improve the performance of the entire organization. A Scanlon plan gives employees a share of the cost savings achieved through increased productivity. A profit-sharing plan gives employees a percentage of the organization's profits.

83. B: Poor communication between management and employees is a common problem during the growth phase of the organizational life cycle. In this phase, the organization often adds new layers of management, and so employees who previously had unfettered access to their superiors may find it difficult to get immediate feedback. This can be alienating for veteran employees. Outsourcing is more typical of the initial phase of the lifecycle, when the organization has yet to create its own departments to handle operations. Excessive bureaucracy and the resulting inefficiencies are common in mature and declining organizations. Finally, an inability to respond quickly to market changes tends to beset an organization after it has stopped growing and entered its decline phase.

84. A: Local epidemics. Working in a foreign country can be very difficult emotionally and psychologically. The more "foreign" the country, the harder it tends to be. However, even moving to a First World capital such as London or Paris may be very difficult. Homesickness on the part of the employee or a spouse or child (or children) is one of the most common reasons for employees returning back home. Culture shock, especially in more exotic locations, is another. Local epidemics are not.

85. D: The 1965 amendments to the Immigration and Nationality Act of 1965 established that the United States gives preferential treatment to those prospective immigrants who have special skills. Until these amendments were passed, some nationalities received preferential treatment. The 1965 amendments made it illegal to use national origin, race, or heritage as a factor in immigration decisions.

86. A: Creating retention plans is a strategic function of the human resources department. This activity is considered strategic because it is concerned with maintaining an optimal workforce over the long term. Recruiting new employees is more of an operational function, in that it is a practical application of the organization's strategic planning. Insuring compliance with federal regulations and maintaining the confidentiality of employee data are considered administrative functions, because they are part of the normal course of business for a human resources department.

87. C: The expectation that employees will meet a minimum standard of effort and competence in their work is known as the duty of diligence. This duty is a part of common law. In other words, within a legal setting, employees are considered to be at fault when they fail to work towards this minimum standard. This presumption is valid in situations that are not otherwise covered in case law.

88. A: Gross profit is calculated by subtracting the cost of goods sold from total sales revenue. The cost of goods sold is the funds that have been expended on materials and labor to create products.

89. C: The Securities Exchange Act of 1934 led to the creation of generally accepted accounting principles (GAAP). This set of accounting standards was developed by the American Institute of Certified Public Accountants. For decades, the AICPA's standards were mandatory for publicly held companies in the United States. In the past few years, however, the Securities Exchange Commission has allowed some businesses to use the standard created by the International Accounting Standards Board.

90. C: Green belts do not work full-time on quality management; they spend some of their time pursuing other organizational initiatives. Green belts may be training to become black belts, who do spend all of their time on quality management issues, usually in a single department. One of the key features of Six Sigma is measurement of defects on the per-million instead of the traditional per-thousand basis. The define, measure, analyze, improve, and control (DMAIC) model of Six Sigma has become perhaps its most recognizable feature.

91. A: Sandra's next step is to research possible systems. Since she has obtained a needs analysis, she should have a good idea of the appropriate system for her business. However, her business may not be able to afford the best possible human resources information system. Sandra's next step will be to shop around for the best value. Answer choices B, C, and D represent steps that she will need to take later in the process.

92. B: The lost time rate is calculated by dividing the number of lost time accidents by 200,000. The number 200,000 is chosen because it is the number of hours worked by a hundred employees (given forty hours a week and fifty weeks a year). Answer choice A is the formula for calculating the lost work day index (LWDI). For this measure, only those days lost to personal injury are counted. Answer choice C is the formula for the OSHA recordable rate. Lost time rate, LWDI, and OSHA recordable rate are the most common methods of calculating the safety of a work site.

93. A: The Age Discrimination in Employment Act requires that any employee records related to charges of discrimination must be retained until the charges are resolved. Once the charges are resolved, records may be expunged. The Age Discrimination in Employment Act was passed with the intention of helping older people find jobs. It required businesses to declare any reasons for failing to hire older workers at an appropriate rate.

94. C: Byron will use a simple linear regression. A simple linear regression is good for examining the relationship between two variables. In this case, Byron wants to look at the relationship between the advertising budget and sales. A trend analysis, on the other hand, focuses on a single variable. A ratio considers the relationship between two variables, but it is more aimed at establishing a traditional benchmark then in learning more about the relationship. Finally, a multiple linear regression analyzes the relationships among more than two variables.

95. B: The primary result of *Faragher v. City of Boca Raton* (1998) was that an adverse TEA need only be implied for harassment to be actionable. This case centered on two female lifeguards who claimed that they were sexually harassed even after reporting this problem to a supervisor. The Supreme Court declared that harassment does not need to be explicit to be a violation of the law.

96. D: The Family and Medical Leave Act defines a "key employee" as any employee whose salary is in the top 10% at the company. Businesses are not required to promise key employees they will be able to return to their position or an equivalent position after FMLA leave. The intention of this exception in the Family Medical Leave Act is to prevent businesses from suffering significant economic injury. However, the FMLA encourages businesses to find ways to grant leave wherever possible.

- 38 -

97. C: The fellow servant rule prevented employees from being compensated when their injury was caused by a colleague. As the phrase suggests, this notion dates back to the time when workers were entirely uncompensated. In the past century, the legal system has begun to recognize that workers require more protection than is provided by relics of common law like the fellow servant rule.

98. B: This is not a work-related illness because the influenza exposure occurred away from work. Of course, it is not always possible to ascertain when exposure occurred, but the mere fact that symptoms began at work is not enough to make this illness work-related.

99. C: According to the Pregnancy Discrimination Act of 1978, employers should treat pregnancy like a short-term disability. The Pregnancy Discrimination Act is an amendment to Title VII. Pregnant women are entitled to all of the benefits and accommodations due to the disabled.

100. D: Paying bribes to foreign officials for favors or access. The Foreign Corrupt Practices Act of 1977 has two main provisions. One of them requires full accounting transparency from companies operating in foreign countries. The other prohibits anyone from bribing a foreign official. In many countries, government officials at all levels consider taking bribes from foreign companies to be standard operating procedure.

101. A: In *Taylor v. Progress Energy, Inc.* (2007), the Supreme Court ruled that employees may not waive their Family and Medical Leave Act rights in a severance agreement. Indeed, the ruling states that employees may neither waive nor be induced to waive any of their FMLA rights.

102. D: A realistic job preview should be used when employee replacement costs are high. If it is expensive to hire and train new employees, it is important to maximize the number of new employees who stay with the organization. A realistic job preview winnows out recruits who are less likely to thrive. The other answer choices are scenarios in which a realistic job preview would not be appropriate. When unemployment is high, recruits will be less likely to decline an unsuitable job, because they will doubt their ability to find another. When recruits have access to plenty of information about the job, a realistic job preview is unnecessary. When the selection ratio is high (there are few applicants relative to the number of jobs available), an organization may not be able to afford scaring away potential employees.

103. C: The Revenue Act of 1978 created 401(k) plans for employees. This act also created flexible spending accounts, so that employees could spend untaxed income on medical expenses and then receive reimbursement.

104. B: The government would not consider the location of the company when evaluating a claim that complying with ADA regulations would constitute an undue hardship. The government does issue some exceptions to the ADA in cases where compliance would significantly impair a business' viability. However, the precise location of the business should not have any effect.

105. A: For every ten-hour week Deirdre works, she uses ¼ of an FMLA leave week. This is calculated by dividing the number of hours off in her reduced schedule by the number of hours in her normal schedule. Because she has three weeks left of FMLA leave, Deirdre may work twelve weeks of this reduced schedule before her leave expires.

106. B: The United States Patent Act does not recognize structure patents. The three types of patents recognized in the United States are design, utility, and plant. A design pattern, which may last no more than 14 years, protects original manufacturing designs. A utility patent, which may last no more than 20 years, protects original processes, machines, and material constructions. A plant

- 39 -

patent, which may last no more than 20 years, protects original, asexually reproduced plant varieties.

107. C: Derek should arrange the seats in the classroom style. In this style, participants are placed behind desks facing towards the front of the room. This seating arrangement is most appropriate for presentations delivered by a single person, especially when the participants will need to be making notes. In conference-style seating, participants are placed around a large square table. In the U-shaped seating style, participants are placed around three sides of a large table, and the presenter stands on the fourth side. In the Chevron style of seating, participants are placed in rows that face the front of the room at an angle, so that they are facing both the presenter and, to a lesser extent, one another.

108. C: A presentation is a passive method of training. Passive training methods are so designated because the participants are only required to listen, read, or pay attention. In a case study, the participants must strategize a response to a hypothetical situation. In vestibule training, employees participate in a simulation of complex or hazardous tasks. In a seminar, participants engage in a productive conversation with the presenter.

109. A: Employees who are terminated for gross misconduct receive no COBRA coverage. This is really the only circumstance in which employees may be denied COBRA coverage. Even when an employee becomes eligible for Social Security benefits, he still receives COBRA coverage for 18 months. An employee who is terminated for reasons other than gross misconduct also continues to receive coverage for 18 months.

110. D: *Electromation, Inc. v. NLRB* (1992) determined that compensating employees for participation in work committees is not a violation of the National Labor Relations Act. This case began when changes to a company's compensation policy were criticized by employees. The company's management allowed the employees to form committees and try to come up with solutions. However, the NLRB determined that management had too much influence in these committees. The ruling suggested, however, that compensating employees for their participation would not necessarily prejudice the proceedings.

111. C: Quality selection is not one of the quality management phases identified by Joseph M. Juran. According to Juran, quality management begins with planning that takes into consideration the most important factors in quality. Quality control is the system that makes sure processes adhere to quality planning. Finally, quality improvements are continuous increases in the standard of organizational performance.

112. A: A seniority-based compensation system is typical of unionized workplaces. One reason for this is that the compensation system of a unionized business is based on negotiation between the employer and the union, rather than on internal measures of performance. One complaint about unions is that by encouraging a seniority system of compensation, they encourage complacency.

113. D: The FrogTech Company is experiencing wage compression. Wage compression exists when new employees make either more money than existing employees or more money than existing employees did when they were hired. For obvious reasons, wage compression can create resentment and conflict in the workforce. Some businesses prevent wage compression by periodically adjusting salary increase rates for existing employees.

114. A: The final step in a job pricing exercise is a salary range recommendation. Job pricing is an exercise for determining the appropriate salary for a new or modified position. It begins by fully defining the job description. The next step is to obtain a relevant salary survey and analyze the

compensation for similar positions. The final step is to recommend a range of salaries, from which executives can choose.

115. B: It is legal for the employee to be searched, but the search should be performed by a law enforcement officer. Body searches are allowed so long as they are conducted for legitimate business reasons. Of course, before requesting a body search the employer should try other means of resolving the situation.

116. C: Goodwill from local citizens and authorities. The geocentric approach to international staffing relies on expatriates to fill foreign positions. This is sometimes a necessity, and there are many benefits to companies who take this approach, but local goodwill is not usually one of them. Local government and citizens often resent when multinational corporations fill local positions with people from the home country.

117. C: The accession rate compares the number of new employees to the total number of employees. This metric indicates whether an organization is experiencing too much or too little turnover. Human resources departments use the accession rate to identify focus areas for their recruiting and retention efforts.

118. A: The founding idea of quality improvement, as espoused by W. Edwards Deming, is that the customer is the ultimate judge of quality. This simple insight, made in the early 1940s, radically changed the way business has been done thereafter. Before Deming, businesses relied on their own metrics and assessments of product quality. After him, they began to ask their customers about what constitutes quality, and make changes accordingly.

119. A: A checklist is a rating method of performance appraisal. In a checklist system, the various elements of the job description are listed, and the employee receives a check mark for each element he performs with competence. This is considered a rating system because the number of checks can be converted into a score, which makes it possible to compare employees. In a field appraisal, someone besides the employee's supervisor observes and reports on the employee's performance. In an essay appraisal, the evaluator writes a short prose passage about the employee's performance. In a critical incident review, the supervisor discusses the especially positive and negative aspects of the employee's performance.

120. C: The HAY system classifies jobs according to knowledge, accountability, and problem solving. This system, which was developed in 1943, is a form of point factor grading. A job's accountability is the degree to which other members of the organization rely on that employee.

121. D: Inability to identify the advantages of change is a primary reason for the failure of total quality management programs. If managers are unable to convey the intended benefits of a new program, employees are less likely to comply with the new standards and regulations. Micromanagement by employees at all levels is a common characteristic of total quality management programs during the implementation phase. These programs are comprehensive, and require the participation of employees at all levels. Total quality management experts would deny that it is possible to overemphasize core objectives, since TQM depends on isolation of key production components and constant attention to improvement. Finally, failure to use ISO 9000 standards does not cause TQM efforts to fail, since there are a number of other standard systems available. Indeed, many industries have special standards that are more appropriate.

122. A: People and production are on the axes of the Blake-Mouton managerial grid. The Blake-Mouton managerial grid is a tool for assessing leadership. It simplifies this complex subject by reducing leadership to its focus on people and its focus on production. In some cases, attention to

- 41 -

one of these factors will necessitate inattention to the other. This model suggests, however, that the best leaders are those who maximize their concern for both people and production.

123. C: The Department of Labor prefers that businesses use positive time reporting with regard to the time worked by employees who are nonexempt under the Fair Labor Standards Act. This method is considered better because it gives a clear indication of the hours worked, without the need for any calculation. For instance, in the other acceptable method, exception reporting, the business establishes a baseline for time worked and only notes deviations from the baseline. This requires the DOL to consider both the baseline and the exceptions. Positive time reporting is simpler.

124. D: Golden life jacket. This kind of arrangement is known as a golden life jacket. A golden parachute is a compensation package an executive is entitled to if an acquiring company lets him go. A golden handshake is a promise of substantial compensation by a prospective or current employer if an executive is fired or laid off. Golden handcuffs are designed to incentivize top executives to stay with a company for an extended period of time, either by offering substantial benefits that only kick in after a certain length of time, or by imposing large penalties (such as being required to return bonuses) if the executives leave before an agreed upon date.

125. B: The Health Insurance Portability and Accountability Act of 1996 made it illegal to discriminate on the basis of health. This act is an amendment to the Employee Retirement Income Security Act of 1972. It also made it harder for insurers to deny coverage based on pre-existing conditions.

126. A: Interviews conducted by the researcher would be considered primary research. Primary research is distinguished by having been conducted by the researcher. Secondary research, on the other hand, is created by someone else. In most cases, it is good to have a mixture of primary and secondary research.

127. C: *Bates v. United Parcel Service* (2006) is the most relevant case to Phil's situation. The ruling in this case established that the company bears the burden of proving that a standard is necessary, even if the candidate is otherwise unqualified. Phil could cite this case to force the employer to justify its standard.

128. C: In a matrix organization, each employee reports to two managers: a product manager and a functional manager. That is, each employee reports to someone responsible for overseeing the development of a particular product, and someone responsible for overseeing certain types of employees. Matrix organizations require a great deal of cooperation and communication.

129. D: Jared is practicing transformational leadership. A transformational leader capitalizes on the good relationships in the group, and acts more as a model than a guide. Transformational leaders create an environment in which employees can improve themselves.

130. A: This situation could be illustrated by a plateau learning curve. In this model, the learner makes rapid progress at first, but learning then slows almost to a halt. A plateau learning curve might occur when a task is easy to become competent at but difficult to master, or when a skill is easy to acquire but rarely practiced.

131. C: If no employees volunteer to accompany the CSHO on her tour of the building, she will interview employees about their working conditions. It is standard procedure for the CSHO to be escorted by an employee, but if this is impossible for some reason, the CSHO continues the

Copyright © Mometrix Media. You have been licensed one copy of this document for personal use only. Any other reproduction or redistribution is strictly prohibited. All rights reserved.

inspection in the most effective way possible. The company will not be penalized for failing to provide an escort.

132. A: In a fertilizer manufacturer, the research and development department is likely to be distinct from the marketing department. As a general rule, the more technologically sophisticated and complex the product, the greater distinction between the R&D and marketing departments. The development of useful and safe fertilizers requires a great deal of experimentation and technical knowledge. Therefore, it is more likely that a fertilizer manufacturer would have a special department for creating and refining products. For a toy manufacturer, publisher, or clothing manufacturer, product development is largely stimulated by the demands of the consumer, so it makes more sense for the marketing department to be loosely involved in research and development.

133. D: The ADDIE model outlines the components of instructional design. The name stands for analysis, design, development, implementation, and evaluation. These are the steps in the creation of an effective training program. They are very similar to the steps in other quality management programs. Because evaluation is the final step, the ADDIE model indicates that improvement should be ongoing.

134. B: Quarterly bonuses based on share price. Tying an executive's pay to share prices in the near future creates a strong incentive for him or her to take actions that aren't good for the company in the long term but can drive the price of the company's stock higher. A golden parachute would not be a risk to a company at all, as it would be paid by another entity in a hostile takeover. A defined contribution pension plan poses no long-term risk to a company at all. LEAPS, or long-term equity anticipation securities, are stock options with expiration dates a year or two down the road. These are less likely to create a perverse incentive than answer choice b.

135. A: This is not considered a work-related injury because vehicle accidents that occur on company property are not considered work-related under the Occupational Health and Safety Act. If Sven had sustained this injury while driving somewhere in a company vehicle or in the pursuit of company business, the accident would be considered work-related.

136. B: One provision of the Fair Labor Standards Act of 1938 is that overtime pay must be 1.5 times the normal hourly wage. Employers may give compensatory time off in lieu of overtime pay. An employee should receive 1.5 times as much compensatory time off as he has worked in overtime. The FLSA established that children may only work limited hours, that the maximum work week is 40 hours, and that some previous compensation laws remain valid.

137. C: When the federal and state minimum wages are different, the higher wage takes precedence. This policy is part of the Fair Labor Standards Act. As of July 2009, federal minimum wage was set at $7.25 an hour. Unless they are exempt for some reason, employees are owed at least minimum wage for all compensable time.

138. A: The executive does not need to pay for the right to reference this work, because *Macbeth* is in the public domain. According to the Copyright Act of 1976, original works are protected for seventy years after the death of the author. Obviously, Shakespeare has been deceased for much longer than that, so the executive does not need to pay royalties.

139. C: The four Ps of marketing are product, price, place, and promotion. Product refers to the characteristics, appearance, and specifications of the item or service being sold. Price refers to the art of maximizing profits by establishing the right cost for the product. Placement refers to the

venues in which the product or service will be sold. Finally, promotion refers to the set of advertising and public relations activities designed to stimulate sale of the product.

140. B: In *Griggs v. Duke Power* (1971), the Supreme Court ruled that job requirements must be demonstrably related to the job. This case was the result of a complaint brought by the black employees of a Duke Power, an energy company in North Carolina. The Supreme Court that Title VII forbade Duke Power from using aptitude tests to keep black employees from a faster promotional track. Even though there was no clear reason for black candidates to score lower on the test, the Court declared that any measure that furthered discrimination was prohibited.

141. B: A company's total rewards packages might lag the market if the company is trying to establish itself in a new area. For instance, if a company simply wants to get a small toehold in a particular market, it may not view hiring top job candidates as a worthwhile enterprise. Of course, if total rewards packages continue to lag the market over a long interval, the company's performance is likely to suffer. However, many fledgling companies have no other choice but to offer lower wages and benefits to new employees at first. Many of these companies do so openly and promise the new employees that their compensation will rise above the market average once the business takes off.

142. D: The Youngblood Company's arrangement is known as a health purchasing alliance. This gives smaller businesses more purchasing power and leverage in negotiations with health insurance providers. In an administrative services only plan, the employer creates a claim fund and then hires an insurance company to manage it. In a third party administrator plan, a business besides the employer or the insurance company handles claims. In a partially self-funded plan, employers only provide a certain amount of coverage. This type of plan ensures that a small business will not be ruined by a single large claim.

143. C: The Greendale Company should ask the IRS for a private letter ruling. Private letter rulings are a courtesy provided by the Internal Revenue Service. When a company is uncertain about the tax implications of a proposed change, it may submit the details to the IRS and receive an estimate. In the long run, the effort expended by the IRS on private letter rulings obviates the need for more work cleaning up unanticipated messes.

144. A: Arranging for temporary employees to be hired by an agency and then sent to work at one's business is known as payrolling. This is a way to avoid the administrative costs of hiring and filling out paperwork for new employees. The temp agency usually requests payment for rendering this service.

145. B: In *Taxman v. Board of Education of Piscataway* (1993), the Court of Appeals for the Third Circuit ruled that protected classes may not be given preferential treatment during layoffs if they have not been discriminated against or underrepresented before. This case was based on a New Jersey school board's decision to lay off a white employee instead of a black colleague with the exact same amount of seniority. The white teacher charged reverse discrimination, and the Third Circuit agreed that the school board's decision was a violation of Title VII. This case was settled before it could reach the Supreme Court on appeal.

146. D: This would not be considered a work-related illness because the food was prepared at home for personal consumption. If the tuna sandwich had been provided by Hubert's employer, his illness would be considered work-related. It does not matter that Hubert ate the sandwich or became sick at the workplace.

147. A: In Victor Vroom's expectancy theory, the reasoned decision to work is called valence. According to this theory, people make a rational calculation of the reward they anticipate receiving in exchange for doing some amount of work. If this reward is deemed sufficient, the person will do the work. Expectancy is the initial assessment of whether the work can be done. Instrumentality is the assessment of the reward.

148. D: Payroll systems are not always the responsibility of the human resources department. In some organizations, payroll is handled by the finance department. The other answer choices are true statements.

149. C: The Uniform Guidelines on Employee Selection Procedures declare that employers must use the selection tool that has the least adverse impact on protected classes. Of course, this provision is only applicable when the employer has access to more than one selection tool. When there is no other option, employers may use selection tools that adversely impact protected classes. According to the UGESP, an adverse impact exists when the selection rate for a protected class is 4/5 or less of the normal selection rate.

150. C: Unions may not participate in secondary boycotts. A secondary boycott occurs when the union tries to make the employer stop doing business with a third party. The other answer choices are false statements.

151. B: According to Feldman's model of organizational socialization, new employees confirm or dismiss their pre-hiring expectations during the encounter stage. Feldman outlined three major stages in organizational socialization: anticipatory socialization, encounter, and change and acquisition. During anticipatory socialization, the potential new employee first learns about the organization. During the encounter stage, the recruit formally commits to joining the organization and becomes a part of it. During the change and acquisition stage, the new employee assimilates to the organizational culture.

152. A: An assisted-living facility would be the most likely of these businesses to have an outbreak of tuberculosis. Tuberculosis is an airborne disease, and spreads quickly in places where people work closely together. An assisted-living facility, where people share the same space and breathe the same air every day, is an excellent breeding ground for TB.

153. A: Immigrant visas are allocated by the federal government on a first come, first served basis. This principle was established by the 1965 amendments to the Immigration and Nationality Act of 1952. There is some preferential treatment for immigrants with special skills. However, work experience is not a factor in visa decisions.

154. D: Wealth is not one of the sources of motivation identified in McClelland's acquired needs theory. According to McClelland, people are driven to pursue achievement, affiliation, or power. Those who seek achievement will take some risks and listen to constructive criticism. However, these people want to ensure that they have responsibility for their work, because having a sense of ownership over the completed task is important for them. People who are motivated by affiliation seek to be accepted by their colleagues and peers. These people should not be isolated. People who seek power want to exert control over people or processes.

155. A: The Office of Federal Contract Compliance Programs prefers that data related to employee race and ethnicity be generated by self-reporting. In other words, it is best if employees indicate their own race or ethnicity, as often happens during the hiring process. Self-reported data is more accurate, and is less likely to be influenced by a desire to demonstrate diversity.

156. C: In a collective bargaining agreement, a union shop clause requires all new employees to join the union within a defined interval. In all industries except construction, this interval must be at least thirty days. In construction, it must be at least a week. A maintenance of membership clause requires employees who choose to join the union to remain enrolled until the union contract expires. However, this clause does not force employees to join the union in the first place. A closed shop clause requires any new employees to join the union. A contract administration clause contains all the administrative details.

157. B: Handing out documents supplementary to lecture materials would help reduce information overload during orientation. Though it may seem that giving new employees more material to look over would contribute to information overload, research has suggested that employees are better able to understand complex subjects when they receive instruction in multiple modes. A focus on the positive aspects of the organization would not necessarily decrease information overload. Conducting a program in one installment would be more likely to overwhelm new employees. Finally, failing to allow employees to raise questions and concerns after a presentation will contribute to information overload.

158. A: In a team-based model of career development, employee movement is generally lateral. The members of a work team are on the same level, and so position change is not generally considered as promotion or demotion. Some organizations encourage this sort of lateral movement because it gives employees a broader set of skills and reduces burnout.

159. B: Approximately $99,000. Under the IRS guidelines for the Foreign Earned Income Exclusion, an American citizen who spends at least 330 days in a foreign country (or countries) may exclude $99,200 of her income from taxation. These are 2014 numbers, which will change, as the number is indexed to the inflation rate.

160. C: One consequence of the Sarbanes-Oxley Act is that CEOs may be punished for fraudulent financial reports. This act was passed in 2002 after several large corporations, most notably Enron, collapsed under the weight of unethical accounting and executive mismanagement. The intention of the Sarbanes-Oxley Act was to make top officials culpable for dishonest and reckless accounting. The act explicitly forbade employees from trading stocks during pension fund blackout periods, and asserted that companies must have their stock appraised by a certified external organization. The act also declared that audit partner assignments must alternate every five years.

161. A: The company being merged with another in a hostile takeover. While all major corporate restructuring events are likely to lead to uncertainty on the part of employees and lower morale, some have a more powerful effect than others. Rumors of the company being victim of a hostile takeover are extremely bad for employee morale, because the uncertainty will be multiplied if new management takes over. Also, in hostile takeovers it's common for the company or party doing the takeover to boast about how many jobs they intend to cut.

162. B: An intellectual property agreement does not need to include a prohibition against the hiring of current employees by employees who leave the business. Many intellectual property agreements do contain such language, however, commonly known as a nonsolicitation clause. The other answer choices represent the essential components of an intellectual property agreement.

163. C: A leave of absence is considered indirect compensation. Compensation is indirect when it cannot easily be assigned a monetary value. Since an employee is not paid during a leave of absence, granting one is not a direct expense for the company. Of course, the employee's absence

may result in diminished productivity and therefore less revenue for the company, but it is difficult to quantify this loss.

164. D: Marital status. Asking about marital status is off limits for employers. This applies to the mergers and acquisitions (M&A) process, as well as to the initial hiring process. Asking such questions is considered a violation of the employee's (or applicant's) privacy.

165. C: The components of the four-dimensional model of management are functions, roles, targets, and styles. In this model, managers have six functions: training and development; persuasive communication; influence and control; forecasting and planning; personal area of expertise; and administration. Managers also have four roles: innovator, evaluator, motivator, and director. Managers have five targets: peers, subordinates, external, superiors, and self. Finally, managers have an indeterminate number of styles, related to the particular personality and approach of the manager.

166. D: A 401(k) contribution is a voluntary deduction from gross earnings. That is, employees are not required to have this money taken out of their paycheck. The other answer choices are statutory deductions, meaning they are required by law.

167. A: In binding arbitration, both parties agree to accept whatever decision is reached by the third party judge. Compulsory arbitration, meanwhile, exists when the terms of a contract dictate that any future disputes will be settled through arbitration. Constructive confrontation is a system for handling disputes within an organization, usually by dividing them into their central and peripheral elements. Ad hoc arbitration is a one-time dispute resolution aimed at handling one particular problem.

168. A: When one company acquires another, the first step for the acquiring company's human resources department is a survey of the workforce in both organizations. The goal is to identify redundant or conflicting positions. It may be that some of the employees in the acquired organization will need to be let go. Human resources departments will need to review the acquired organization's collective bargaining agreements and ensure compliance with OSHA regulations, but these activities should be performed subsequent to the workforce survey.

169. C: Exit interviews should be conducted by a third party. In many cases, employees will leave an organization because they are not satisfied with it or with the work environment. However, an employee may not feel comfortable sharing these complaints with current members of the organization. Indeed, this reticence may be a result of why they are leaving the organization in the first place. Having exit interviews conducted by a third party ensures that the process will yield more useful information for the organization.

170. D: Statistical power is the extent to which research results accurately identify differences between trained and untrained employees. Of course, researchers want to design a method that will have the maximum statistical power. If the statistical power of the research is low, it is likely that a difference between the trained and untrained employees will pass unnoticed. It can be difficult to obtain powerful statistical results from research into employee training in large part because the methods of assessing performance are so subjective.

171. D: The supervisors at Flanders Company are practicing extinction, though they are most likely unaware of doing so. Extinction occurs when the positive reinforcement that followed a behavior ceases, and the behavior gradually ceases as well. Punishment is a negative consequence to a behavior. The absence of positive reinforcement is not considered punishment. Positive

reinforcement is a reward, while negative reinforcement is the removal of a punishment. Positive and negative reinforcement are both used to encourage certain behaviors.

172. C: A corporate university is an extensive training program administered by a corporation to existing employees. Rather than rely on local colleges to keep their employees up to date, many organizations have created in-house training programs. Corporate universities often have detailed curricula and "professors" whose only job is to maintain the skills and competence of existing employees. Those who complete a program at a corporate university may be eligible for a raise or promotion. Corporate universities are able to be much more specific and targeted in their instruction.

173. B: The employees of Fitch Company have line of sight. Line of sight exists when employees feel that their performance will determine their compensation in the future. Companies in which employees have line of sight tend to have higher levels of performance. A company with an entitlement philosophy rewards employees for seniority. Intrinsic rewards are the pleasures and satisfactions of a job well done. Businesses should seek to maximize the opportunities for creating intrinsic rewards for their employees. A fiduciary responsibility is the duty to handle someone else's affairs, typically with regard to financial matters, with appropriate care.

174. B: The Davis-Bacon Act was the first federal legislation to address minimum wages. This act asserted that all workers on federal public works projects must be paid the standard local wage. Before this law was passed, contractors would make extremely low bids for projects because they paid laborers almost nothing.

175. A: The four styles of leadership identified by the Hersey-Blanchard theory are telling, selling, participating, and delegating. This model was developed by Paul Hersey and Kenneth Blanchard in the late 1970s. The appropriate style of leadership in a particular situation depends on the sophistication and experience of the subordinates. The range, from least sophisticated audience to most, is telling, selling, participating, and delegating. Telling is explicit instruction, while selling is more general encouragement and inspiration. Participating is working alongside employees, and delegating is setting goals and assigning responsibility to others.

Practice Test #2

1. What kind of visa would allow a foreign national already working for your company in her home country to come to the US temporarily to work for the company here?

    a. H-B2
    b. L-1
    c. I-551
    d. F-1

2. A small publishing company has decided to advertise for a new open position within the marketing department. Although the new hire will fall under the leadership of the marketing department, the job itself will require ongoing communication with at least two other departments. As a result, the individual that is hired will have to be able to work well with the leadership of the other departments. With this in mind, which of the following types of interview techniques will be best for screening prospective candidates?

    a. Situational
    b. Behavioral
    c. Functional
    d. Panel

3. A large corporation has raised concerns about the quality of written reports within the company. A cursory review has indicated that many employees, while they have advanced degrees, lack basic writing skills suitable for a corporate environment. The corporation has convened a committee to look into the matter, and the committee has requested input from the human resources professional on the appropriate action to take. What is the primary step that the human resources professional can make to the committee?

    a. Review the resumes of all recent hires for writing courses they have completed
    b. Require that all employees take a brief course to improve writing skills
    c. Develop an internal assessment to test the writing skill level of current employees
    d. Review recent writing samples to determine if employee skills are too low

4. The Immigration Reform and Control Act of 1986 was intended to accomplish four major purposes. Which of the following is not one of these purposes?

    a. Provide amnesty for all illegal immigrants that had been in the United States for at least four years
    b. Make employers responsible for providing documentation to prove the legal immigration status of their employees
    c. Require employers to weight hiring in favor of candidates who were already American citizens
    d. Provide amnesty for agricultural workers who have worked in the United States for many years

5. The development section of a large energy company is in the process of overhauling its risk management program. In particular, the development section expects to assemble a new risk management program that takes previous situations more carefully into account. The head of the development company has contacted the human resources department for advice. What is the role of the human resources professional in this situation?

    a. Provide the development section of the company with documentation that details current legal requirements for risk management
    b. Remain in contact with the department and ensure that the risk management program meets all legal and procedural requirements
    c. Establish parameters for the development section to begin assembling its new risk management program
    d. Recommend a training program for employees of the development section to implement the risk management program

6. A marketing research company has decided to do a little research on its own employees to find out which communication methods work best. The company would like to implement a testing program that follows and reviews employee activities, and they are considering several options. To assist them in making the final decision, the company has forwarded the information to the human resources professional. What is the role of the human resources professional in this situation?

    a. Review the testing tools in advance to ensure they meet all legal and procedural requirements for reliability and fairness
    b. Use current company policy and legal requirements to select the best testing program that may be applied to employees
    c. Assist the company by eliminating testing programs that are not appropriate and may not be used in this type of situation
    d. Recommend that the company develop a new testing program that more closely meets the unique needs of the organization

7. With the training program described in question 6, the marketing research company also has budget constraints to consider. What is the human resources professional's role in budget and costs for this projected company activity?

    a. Assist in preparing a cost-analysis review that will consider the expenses and benefits of each testing option
    b. Research the cost of each testing program to eliminate any options that exceed the budget constraints of the company
    c. Review options to determine if the company can utilize part of the testing program and avoid the full cost
    d. Recommend cost-cutting measures for other company activities to ensure that the necessary training can take place

8. The National Labor Relations Act (NLRA) does not apply to which types of workers?

    a. Administrative
    b. Corporate
    c. Financial
    d. Agricultural

9. Which of the following pieces of legislation made it illegal for a business to discriminate against an employee due to his national origin?

    a. Sarbanes-Oxley Act
    b. Rehabilitation Act
    c. Title VII
    d. HIPAA

10. Which of the following pieces of legislation protects workers against losing their health coverage immediately if they lose their jobs?

    a. Sarbanes-Oxley Act
    b. Rehabilitation Act
    c. Title VII
    d. HIPAA

11. Which of the following is not considered a top-down method of communication delivery?

    a. Posters
    b. Bulletin board postings
    c. Brown bag meetings
    d. Newsletters

12. Which of the following expense items is not typically under the control of the human resources professional?

    a. Supplies
    b. Travel
    c. Maintenance
    d. Raises

13. An athlete or entertainer would fall under which of the following classifications for a visa?

    a. R
    b. P
    c. H
    d. L

14. Within the SMART model, the letters stand for Specific, Measurable, Action-Oriented, _____, and Time-based. What does the "R" stand for?

    a. Reasonable
    b. Reversible
    c. Realistic
    d. Representative

15. Polygraph testing for employment falls under which of the following federal departments?

    a. Department of Labor
    b. Federal Trade Commission
    c. USCIS
    d. Department of Justice

16. Risk is defined as Probability x _____:

    a. Prevention
    b. Occurrence
    c. Avoidance
    d. Consequences

17. *Risk transfer* can typically be effected by doing which of the following?

    a. Reviewing employment policies frequently to avoid the chances of an employee lawsuit
    b. Purchasing employment practices liability insurance to protect a business
    c. Taking advance action to consider potentials for risk and prevent problems from occurring
    d. Being familiar with chances of risk and creating a financial buffer against future costs

18. A second IRCA violation results in which of the following penalties?

    a. Not less than $250 and not more than $1,000 for each unauthorized employee
    b. Not less than $1,000 and not more than $2,000 for each unauthorized employee
    c. Not less than $2,000 and not more than $5,000 for each unauthorized employee
    d. Not less than $5,000 and not more than $10,000 for each unauthorized employee

19. To save costs, a call center located in Ohio has decided to outsource one of its largest departments to a country overseas. The manager of this department, Gina, has the task of informing her employees about this event. She consults the human resources professional, Silvia, about the best approach to take. What advice should Silvia give to Gina?

    a. Recommend that Gina provide all employees with a hand-written note explaining the situation
    b. Recommend that Gina assist employees in finding new positions once their jobs end
    c. Recommend that Gina be honest and share with her employees as many facts as possible
    d. Recommend that Gina petition the call center to retain the department by proving the employees' value

20. Felix is interviewing a candidate for a position in an oil and gas company with locations around the world. As they talk, the candidate mentions his wife. What is an appropriate question that Felix may ask the candidate about his family?

    a. Are you willing to relocate?
    b. Do you and your wife plan to have children?
    c. Do any other family members live with you?
    d. Does your wife also work?

21. In terms of required document retention, which of the following is not covered by Title VII of the Civil Rights Act of 1964?

    a. Apprentice selection records
    b. Employee resumes
    c. Tax deductions
    d. Affirmative action plan

22. Which of the following refers to the measurement of the relationship between the characteristics of each employee and his actual performance in the position?

    a. Construct validity
    b. Criterion validity
    c. Concurrent validity
    d. Content validity

23. While interviewing a candidate, Geraldine notices that the individual's answers seem to be oddly phrased, and Geraldine ultimately notices that the candidate is trying to give her the answers that she wants, rather than offering candid answers. In this case, what type of interview bias is occurring?

    a. Halo effect
    b. Cultural noise
    c. Central tendency
    d. Horn effect

24. Which of the following is not considered a bottom-up method of communication delivery?

    a. Open-door policy
    b. Individual letters
    c. Webcasts
    d. Staff meetings

25. Work schedule documents, covered under the Fair Labor Standards Act (FLSA), should be retained for how many years?

    a. 1
    b. 2
    c. 3
    d. 5

26. Which of the following is not included as a job category under the EEO-1 report?

    a. Sales workers
    b. Service workers
    c. Craft workers
    d. Medical workers

27. Michal is interested in applying for a promotion within the publishing company where she works. What type of application would be most appropriate for the human resources professional to provide in this situation?

    a. Job-specific application
    b. Short-form application
    c. Long-form application
    d. Weighted application

28. Arthur is interviewing candidates for a new position within his department. He will be working closely with the person he hires, so he prefers the interview to feel as comfortable as possible so the two can chat about the job and its requirements. His preferred interview method is to ask a few broad questions and to allow the candidate to answer the questions candidly, with his answers guiding the next questions that Arthur asks. In this situation, what type of interview technique is Arthur using?

    a. Behavioral
    b. Patterned
    c. Directive
    d. Nondirective

29. An automotive plant with 70 employees will be closing within the next six months, and the majority of the workers will be laid off. Based on the requirements of the WARN Act of 1988, how long in advance of the closing is the plant expected to inform the workers of the impending lay-offs?

    a. 30 days
    b. 60 days
    c. 90 days
    d. 120 days

30. Dalton, a human resources professional for an engineering firm, is completing a series of annual reports. During his analysis of employee status, he divides the average number of employees for the year (150) by the number of employees who left the firm during the year (8). He arrives at a rate of 18.75. What is this type of result called?

    a. Accession rate
    b. Replacement cost
    c. Turnover analysis
    d. Quality of hire

31. Which of the following types of analytical tools is used primarily for reviewing a series of random events to locate a potential pattern within them?

    a. Check sheet
    b. Pareto chart
    c. Scatter chart
    d. Histogram

32. All of the following are part of the Six Sigma (DMAIC) philosophy except:

    a. Identify
    b. Control
    c. Define
    d. Measure

33. The "best practice" retention period for employee records that relate to discrimination charges should be how long after the employee is no longer with the company?

    a. 2 years
    b. 5 years
    c. 7 years
    d. 10 years

34. A small restaurant is looking for a new short order cook. Because the job requires that the individual be able to work quickly and efficiently, the restaurant presents candidates with a pre-employment test that will measure how well each completes a variety of food preparation tasks. Which of the following types of tests would be most appropriate?

    a. Cognitive Ability Test
    b. Psychomotor Assessment Test
    c. Physical Assessment Test
    d. Aptitude Test

35. According to the Walsh Healy Public Contracts Act of 1936, what is the contract threshold for government contractors to be required to pay the local minimum wage to employees?

    a. $5,000
    b. $10,000
    c. $15,000
    d. $20,000

36. The Walsh Healy Public Contracts Act of 1936 applies to all types of government contract work except which of the following?

    a. Construction
    b. Technology
    c. Security
    d. Delivery

37. How many complaints about an employer's potential violation of FLSA rules can cause the government to step in and perform an audit of the business?

    a. 1
    b. 2
    c. 3
    d. 5

38. Which of the following is not an acceptable reason for FMLA leave?

    a. Resting during a difficult pregnancy
    b. Caring for a newborn infant
    c. Caring for a partner who is ill
    d. Adopting or fostering a child

39. Which Department of Labor form is appropriate for FMLA regulations that apply to caring for a covered service member?

    a. WH-380-E
    b. WH-380-F
    c. WH-384
    d. WH-385

40. Which of the following is not a valid step in the mediation process?

    a. Structure
    b. Introductions
    c. Opinions
    d. Negotiating

41. A large bank has been experiencing a high rate of unacceptable employee absenteeism. In most cases, employees are claiming sick days when evidence indicates that they are not ill and are, in fact, engaging in a variety of activities. For a number of these employees, the days absent are no longer covered by FMLA, and the bank needs to apply disciplinary actions for excess absenteeism. Unfortunately, a clear inappropriate-absence policy is not within the employee manual, so the bank asks the human resources professional to assist in developing one. Such a policy should contain all of the following except:

    a. Statement about how many sick days each employee receives
    b. Indication of how sick days are counted within the calendar
    c. Information about how each absence is counted in days
    d. Requirement for a doctor's note for each sick day absence

42. Three barriers resulted in the need for the 1991 Glass Ceiling Act. These barriers were internal structural barriers, societal barriers, and which of the following types of barriers?

    a. Governmental
    b. Recruitment
    c. Educational
    d. Corporate

43. Which of the following is the acronym used to describe an exception to any of the anti-discrimination laws for employment?

    a. EEOE
    b. SCIS
    c. EADE
    d. BFOQ

44. The Latin phrase *respondeat superior* translates to which of the following?

    a. Friend of the court
    b. Let the master answer
    c. With connected strength
    d. Thrown to the lions

45. According to FLSA, what is the minimum age for children to be hired for a non-farm job?

    a. 15
    b. 16
    c. 18
    d. 19

46. Which type of testing is not part of the medical examination conditions of ADA and may be required of any candidate?

    a. Polygraph test
    b. Drug screening test
    c. Driving test
    d. Aptitude test

47. Which of the following pieces of legislation does not, at this time, apply to private employers?

    a. Fair Credit Reporting Act of 1970
    b. Immigration and Nationality Act of 1952
    c. Civil Rights Act of 1991
    d. Privacy Act of 1974

48. Which of the following is defined as an attempt to improve overall business operations so that customers benefit from the process?

    a. Workforce expansion
    b. Divestiture
    c. Reengineering
    d. Offshoring

49. Which of the following is defined as a business decision to eliminate a department by laying off employees or moving them to another department?

    a. Workforce expansion
    b. Divestiture
    c. Reengineering
    d. Offshoring

50. Which of the following is not one of the seven recognized racial categories for EEO-1?

    a. Native Hawaiian
    b. Alaska Native
    c. Asian
    d. European

51. Which of the following is not a potential candidate for offshoring?

    a. Accounting
    b. Payroll
    c. Call center
    d. All of the above could potentially be offshored

52. The EEO-1 report must be completed on or before which date each year?

    a. January 31
    b. April 1
    c. June 15
    d. September 30

53. The EEO-1 filing is required of private employers with a minimum of how many employees?

    a. 50
    b. 75
    c. 100
    d. 200

54. The EEO-1 filing applies to all types of employers except which of the following?

    a. Administrative
    b. Banking
    c. Education
    d. Construction

55. Which of the following types of health care plans does not require that patients first contact a "gatekeeper" for medical treatment but allows patients to choose from a broad network?

    a. PPO
    b. POS
    c. HMO
    d. FFS

56. Which of the following types of health care plans does require a "gatekeeper" but also focuses on lower health care costs for patients and care that aims to prevent higher costs later on?

    a. PPO
    b. POS
    c. HMO
    d. FFS

57. Which of the following types of health care plans is generally the most costly for patients but allows them to make their own selection of facilities and physicians?

    a. PPO
    b. POS
    c. HMO
    d. FFS

58. Which of the following is not considered a *voluntary* benefit that employers may provide for employees?

    a. Short-term disability insurance
    b. Vision insurance
    c. Medicare
    d. Life insurance

59. Which of the following is considered an *involuntary* benefit that employers must provide for employees?

    a. Social security
    b. Vacation time
    c. Qualified pension plan
    d. Paid holidays

60. What is the main reason for offshoring?

    a. To cut costs
    b. To open new markets
    c. For tax avoidance
    d. To meet EEOC goals

61. Which of the following pieces of legislation covers the employer's ability to monitor the electronic communications of employees?

    a. FLSA
    b. OSHA
    c. MSHA
    d. ECPA

62. The Motivation/Hygiene Theory (1959) is attributed to which of the following researchers?

    a. Fredrick Herzberg
    b. Clayton Alderfer
    c. Abraham Maslow
    d. Victor Vroom

63. The ERG Theory (1969) is attributed to which of the following researchers?

    a. Fredrick Herzberg
    b. Clayton Alderfer
    c. Abraham Maslow
    d. Victor Vroom

64. The Expectancy Theory (1964) is attributed to which of the following researchers?

    a. Fredrick Herzberg
    b. Clayton Alderfer
    c. Abraham Maslow
    d. Victor Vroom

65. The Hierarchy of Needs Theory (1954) is attributed to which of the following researchers?

    a. Fredrick Herzberg
    b. Clayton Alderfer
    c. Abraham Maslow
    d. Victor Vroom

66. In B.F. Skinner's theory of Operant Conditioning (1957), he provided a list of four strategies for behavioral intervention: Positive Reinforcement, Negative Reinforcement, Punishment, and which of the following?

    a. Termination
    b. Encouragement
    c. Extinction
    d. Actualization

67. Ilsa, a manager of a large municipal department, is generally commended for her hands-on approach and effectiveness. However, she has a tendency to lose her temper with employees when she is under stress, and several complaints have been made. Ilsa's boss Kathryn is making an effort to improve Ilsa's behavior, and she has decided to employ Skinner's theory of Operant Conditioning. Which of the following would be an example of negative reinforcement?

    a. For every employee complaint about Ilsa's bad temper, Kathryn will document the incident with an official warning.
    b. To avoid provoking Ilsa into a bad temper due to stress, Kathryn will review her workload to see if more work can be delegated within the department.
    c. For every week that goes by without an employee complaint, Kathryn will reward Ilsa by documenting the behavior with an official commendation.
    d. For every week that goes by without an employee complaint, Ilsa will not have to meet with Kathryn for a behavioral review.

68. Within the Hersey-Blanchard (1977), there are four leadership styles: Selling, Telling, Delegating, and which of the following?

a. Participating
b. Directing
c. Motivating
d. Guiding

69. Which of the following might be an example of *Transactional Leadership*?

a. A manager sets monthly goals for his department and offers motivational rewards to employees if they accomplish these goals.
b. A manager takes the time to sit down with each employee and assist him in utilizing individual skills within the department.
c. A manager has a series of tasks that need to be completed and assigns each employee a task, based on the employee's particular skill sets.
d. A manager allows employees to determine where they fit best within the department and encourages them to work at their own pace.

70. Lewis is in charge of collecting feedback from employees about a new program that his company has implemented. The company has a number of locations, spread out across four different countries. Which of the following methods of data collection would be most effective for Lewis to employ?

a. Focus group
b. Interviews
c. Questionnaire
d. Observation

71. A SWOT analysis has four parts: Strengths, Weaknesses, Opportunities, and which of the following?

a. Tools
b. Threats
c. Targets
d. Techniques

72. A human resources department is reviewing its current staffing availability and needs. The company is attempting to reduce unnecessary costs and has asked the human resources department to see if any cuts can be made. After a careful review, the human resources manager realizes that the department can make some positive changes. In particular, two of his employees have been requesting reduced hours, and he realizes that they have similar skills and have essentially been doing the same job. What is one option for the employees in this situation?

a. On-call
b. Telecommuting
c. Internship
d. Job-sharing

73. The Fair Labor Standards Act (FLSA) has two significant amendments that have been added since the legislation was first passed in 1938. One of these amendments forbids any type of discrimination based on the employee's gender. Which of the following reflects this amendment?

 a. Portal to Portal Act
 b. Equal Pay Act
 c. Davis Beacon Act
 d. National Labor Relations Act

74. The second of these important amendments to FLSA determined that employers cannot be required to compensate employees who commute long distances to work. Which of the following reflects this amendment?

 a. Portal to Portal Act
 b. Equal Pay Act
 c. Davis Beacon Act
 d. National Labor Relations Act

75. Which of the following is considered the *first* piece of legislation to affect the movement for labor rights within the United States?

 a. Clayton Act
 b. Railway Labor Act
 c. Sherman Anti-Trust Act
 d. Norris-La Guardia Act

76. Which of the following federal agencies is responsible for enforcing corporate governance?

 a. SEC
 b. EEOC
 c. MSHA
 d. OFCCP

77. The Drug-Free Workplace Act of 1988 applies to federal contracts of a minimum of how much?

 a. $50,000
 b. $75,000
 c. $80,000
 d. $100,000

78. Any penalties for failing to comply with the Drug-Free Workplace Act must fall in line with standards that were laid out in which piece of legislation?

 a. Davis Beacon Act
 b. Fair Labor Standards Act
 c. Rehabilitation Act
 d. Service Contract Act

79. OSHA operates under three *primary* expectations for employers. Which of the following is not one of these expectations?

 a. Educate employees about safety in the workplace
 b. Provide employees a safe place to work
 c. Ensure that federal safety standards are met
 d. Ensure that occupational safety standards are met

- 61 -

80. An OSHA violation that is categorized as "other-than-serious" has a maximum fine of how much?

    a. $5,000

    b. $7,000

    c. $10,000

    d. $12,000

81. A repeat OSHA violation has a maximum fine of how much?

    a. $25,000

    b. $40,000

    c. $70,000

    d. $85,000

82. Employers with a minimum of how many employees are required by federal law to complete OSHA forms?

    a. 6

    b. 11

    c. 14

    d. 17

83. Which of the following OSHA forms is intended to be a Summary of Work-Related Injuries and Illnesses?

    a. OSHA Form 300

    b. OSHA Form 300A

    c. OSHA Form 301

    d. OSHA Form 301A

84. Which of the following OSHA forms is intended to be an Injury and Illness Incident Report?

    a. OSHA Form 300

    b. OSHA Form 300A

    c. OSHA Form 301

    d. OSHA Form 301A

85. Which of the following OSHA forms is intended to be a Log of Work-Related Injuries and Illnesses?

    a. OSHA Form 300

    b. OSHA Form 300A

    c. OSHA Form 301

    d. OSHA Form 301A

86. Based on federal recommendations, for how long should OSHA forms be retained by an employer?

    a. 2 years

    b. 3 years

    c. 5 years

    d. 7 years

87. Recent laws now extend privacy standards to employees regarding OSHA forms. Apart from the employee's specific request, in which of the following cases would it be legally advisable to label the employee's file with a case number instead of the employee's name on OSHA Form 300?

    a. An employee develops hepatitis in the workplace
    b. An employee develops the flu after receiving a flu vaccine in the workplace
    c. An employee develops food poisoning in the workplace
    d. An employee receives a head injury in the workplace

88. When a Compliance Safety and Health Officer (CSHO) holds an inspection of a business, all of the following must occur during the inspection except:

    a. Opening conference
    b. Presentation of credentials
    c. Resolution of problem
    d. Tour of facilities

89. Within how many days of receiving a citation must an employer file a Notice of Contest?

    a. 7
    b. 15
    c. 30
    d. 45

90. NIOSH created which of the following programs to assist in responding to employer, as well as employee, concerns about workplace hazards?

    a. HHE
    b. VPP
    c. MSH
    d. MSD

91. The largest number of work-related injuries and health problems in the United States each year belong to which of the following categories?

    a. Job-related stress
    b. Excess physical output
    c. Poor ergonomics
    d. Psychological strain

92. A business with a minimum of how many employees is required by OSHA to provide an Injury and Illness Prevention Plan?

    a. 4
    b. 11
    c. 15
    d. 17

93. All of the following relate specifically to workers' compensation laws for particular industries except:

    a. FECA
    b. BLBA
    c. LHWCA
    d. NLRA

94. Which of the following is defined as an occasion when an employer offers an employee some form of reward for completing an action, and then fails to follow through with that reward?

    a. Fraudulent misrepresentation
    b. Promissory estoppel
    c. Constructive discharge
    d. Duty of good faith

95. Helena is the human resources professional for a large legal firm. The upper management is interested in polling employees about ideas for improvements, but the firm has a solid hierarchy in place. As a result, many of the lower-level employees have confided in Helena that they do not feel comfortable speaking up. Which of the following ideas might Helena recommend to allow employees to voice their opinions without fear of upsetting higher-ranking employees?

    a. Brown bag lunch
    b. Focus group
    c. Email
    d. Suggestion box

96. Which of the following is recognized as a ranking system for businesses to utilize in reviewing employee behavior and ensuring that it meets the established standards?

    a. MBOS
    b. BARS
    c. TQMS
    d. PBTS

97. What is the recommended minimum amount of advance notice that employers should provide employees before a scheduled performance evaluation?

    a. 2 days
    b. 3 days
    c. 5 days
    d. 7 days

98. Which of the following types of employee rating systems usually results in rating employees along a bell curve?

    a. Paired comparison
    b. Forced distribution
    c. Ranking
    d. Nominal scale

99. Which of the following types of employee rating systems is usually better for a smaller group of employees but can be difficult to organize with a larger group?

    a. Paired comparison
    b. Forced distribution
    c. Ranking
    d. Nominal scale

100. In which of the following types of employee rating systems is each employee's performance viewed in the context of another employee's performance?

    a. Paired comparison
    b. Forced distribution
    c. Ranking
    d. Nominal scale

101. A human resources professional is putting together a training session, during which employees will be expected to complete a number of small group activities. What type of seating would be most effective for this training session?

    a. Classroom
    b. Chevron
    c. Banquet
    d. Theater

102. For a different training session, the course will include several video presentations, while the instructor and students will also be expected to interact during the session. What type of seating would be most effective for this training session?

    a. Classroom
    b. Chevron
    c. Banquet
    d. Theater

103. A company-wide training session for a large firm will involve a number of film presentations, but participants—every employee of the firm—will not be expected to interact with one another. What type of seating would be most effective for this training session?

    a. Classroom
    b. Chevron
    c. Banquet
    d. Theater

104. The term *zero defects*, as an ideal performance standard, was developed by which individual?

    a. Crosby
    b. Deming
    c. Juran
    d. Ishikawa

105. The Change Process Theory, attributed to Kurt Lewin, includes all of the following stages for change except:

    a. Moving
    b. Unfreezing
    c. Refreezing
    d. Implementing

106. In which of the following situations would the use of copyrighted material <u>not</u> fall under the definition of *fair use*?

    a. Educational purposes within the organization
    b. Limited copies of the material
    c. Use of a single paragraph from a book
    d. Addition of quoted information into the company motto

107. According to the Immigration Act of 1990, a maximum of how many immigrants may enter under the H-1B status (temporary workers) each year?

    a. 45,000
    b. 50,000
    c. 65,000
    d. 70,000

108. The law HR 4306, passed in 2005, allowed for I-9 forms to be stored by which of the following forms of media?

    a. Microfilm
    b. Paper
    c. PDF
    d. Microfiche

109. Within how many days of employment must a business complete the I-9 form for new employees?

    a. 1 day
    b. 3 days
    c. 5 days
    d. 7 days

110. The Immigration Reform and Control Act (IRCA) of 1986 applies to businesses with minimum of how many employees?

    a. 4
    b. 7
    c. 10
    d. 12

111. Which of the following is defined as the knowledge employees have about how their work behavior affects their compensation?

    a. Entitlement philosophy
    b. Line of sight
    c. Total rewards strategy
    d. Organizational culture

- 66 -

112. Which of the following scenarios represents a legitimate exemption status for an employer?

   a. The high school football coach of a large high school is exempt from overtime requirements due to taking students to out-of-town games

   b. A large farm that employs teenagers during the summer months is exempt from child labor requirements

   c. The firefighters in a twelve-person department of a medium-sized town are exempt from minimum wage requirements

   d. The police officers in the four-person police department of a small town is exempt from overtime requirements

113. All of the following are acceptable salary deductions for exempt employees except:

   a. Unpaid leave under FMLA

   b. Suspensions for two days due to inappropriate workplace behavior

   c. During the first week of employment when employee works a full week

   d. To offset an employee's military pay

114. A secretive Wall Street billionaire suddenly begins buying large amounts of your stock. This is most likely a signal that he is preparing to launch:

   a. A hostile takeover of your company

   b. A massive short sale of your company's stock

   c. A friendly acquisition of your company

   d. An SEC investigation of your company

115. What is the youngest age at which children may legally work, under certain conditions, as stipulated by FLSA?

   a. 13

   b. 14

   c. 15

   d. 16

116. Children as young as the age indicated in question 115 may work in all of the following types of jobs except:

   a. Farming

   b. Retail

   c. Technical

   d. Administrative

117. Which of the following is defined as pay legally required whether or not an employer has immediate work available for an employee?

   a. Geographic pay

   b. On-call pay

   c. Reporting pay

   d. Call-back pay

118. Which of the following is defined as pay provided for employees who respond to a work situation at short notice?

    a. Geographic pay
    b. On-call pay
    c. Reporting pay
    d. Call-back pay

119. Which of the following is defined as pay provided for employees who must come into work beyond the scheduled work hours?

    a. Geographic pay
    b. On-call pay
    c. Reporting pay
    d. Call-back pay

120. In the HAY system, which of the following is not a defined factor for job evaluation?

    a. Knowledge
    b. Accountability
    c. Review
    d. Problem solving

121. Which of the following is defined as an increased rate of pay for a new employee, due to that employee's education or experience?

    a. Wage compression
    b. Compa-ration
    c. Range placement
    d. Pay structure

122. What is the established radius for which FMLA applies to employees working for private employers?

    a. 30 miles
    b. 50 miles
    c. 75 miles
    d. 85 miles

123. Similar to question 122, FMLA applies to private employers with a minimum of how many employees?

    a. 15
    b. 20
    c. 35
    d. 50

124. Which of the following is identified as the "eligibility, rights, and responsibilities notice" for employees regarding FMLA?

    a. WH-380
    b. WH-381
    c. WH-382
    d. WH-383

125. Which of the following is identified as a "designation notice" to inform employees about FMLA requirements for factors such as a required medical certification or a required fitness-for-duty certification?

    a. WH-380
    b. WH-381
    c. WH-382
    d. WH-383

126. In terms of "foreseeable leave" for FMLA rights, how long in advance must an employee notify his employer?

    a. 15 days
    b. 30 days
    c. 45 days
    d. 60 days

127. If the leave is foreseeable but the employee fails to provide his employer with appropriate advance notice, for how long after the start of the leave may the employer delay the employee's FMLA coverage?

    a. 15 days
    b. 30 days
    c. 45 days
    d. 60 days

128. Which of the following is not considered a type of FMLA leave?

    a. Continuous
    b. Reduced
    c. Permanent
    d. Intermittent

129. The role of the human resources professional regarding FMLA rules includes all of the following except:

    a. Being familiar with FMLA requirements and changes
    b. Educating those in management about FMLA rules
    c. Developing an FMLA documentation policy for the company
    d. Working to avoid simultaneous FMLA leave among employees

130. Which of the following pieces of legislation does not play a role in regulating voluntary benefits programs?

    a. ERISA
    b. HIPAA
    c. COBRA
    d. VEVRA

131. In *graded vesting*, how much must be vested after three years of employment?

    a. 10%
    b. 15%
    c. 20%
    d. 25%

132. In *cliff vesting*, 100% must be vested after how long?

  a. 2 years
  b. 3 years
  c. 4 years
  d. 5 years

133. A culture in which people tend to have fewer but stronger social ties is a:

  a. Level context culture
  b. High context culture
  c. Low context culture
  d. Graduated context culture

134. Which of the following represents an important change that occurred with the 2006 passing of the Pension Protection Act (PPA)?

  a. The age limit for vesting in the pension plan was lowered
  b. Employees must now choose to opt out of the program
  c. Part of the pension plan is now subject to higher income tax
  d. Employees over the age of 50 may increase their catch-up contributions

135. Edith, an employee of a small business, is eligible for COBRA coverage through her employer. As it turns out, though, Edith is late of making payments toward her COBRA coverage, and the employer is considering the option of discontinuing the coverage. Edith's employer may choose to discontinue her COBRA coverage if her payments are not received within how many days of being due?

  a. 15 days
  b. 30 days
  c. 45 days
  d. 60 days

136. How much COBRA coverage is allowed after a divorce occurs?

  a. 0 months
  b. 18 months
  c. 29 months
  d. 36 months

137. How much COBRA coverage is allowed after an employee is terminated due to being disabled?

  a. 0 months
  b. 18 months
  c. 29 months
  d. 36 months

138. How much COBRA coverage is allowed for a dependent child who no longer falls under standard health coverage?

  a. 0 months
  b. 18 months
  c. 29 months
  d. 36 months

139. How much COBRA coverage is allowed if an employee is terminated due to "gross misconduct"?

    a. 0 months
    b. 18 months
    c. 29 months
    d. 36 months

140. Within how many days of a divorce or legal separation must an employer be notified to ensure COBRA coverage?

    a. 15 days
    b. 30 days
    c. 45 days
    d. 60 days

141. Which of the following types of deferred compensation plans offers employees a fixed annual percentage and thus is best in a company that has fairly consistent annual earnings?

    a. Profit-sharing
    b. Money purchase
    c. Cash balance
    d. Target benefit

142. Which of the following types of deferred compensation plans, also known as a discretionary contribution plan, is considered to be best in a company that has highly variable annual profits?

    a. Profit-sharing
    b. Money purchase
    c. Cash balance
    d. Target benefit

143. Which of the following types of deferred compensation plans is considered "portable" because employees can remove the money from the plan and convert the payment into other forms?

    a. Profit-sharing
    b. Money purchase
    c. Cash balance
    d. Target benefit

144. Which of the following is not considered a statutory deduction?

    a. Union dues
    b. Social Security
    c. State income tax
    d. Federal income tax

145. Which of the following agencies is responsible for enforcing the rights of veterans in the workplace?

    a. EEOC
    b. DOJ
    c. DOL
    d. OFCCP

146. According to Title III of the Consumer Credit Protection Act of 1968, up to which percentage of an employee's income may be garnished for child support payments, if the employee is responsible for supporting a child or a spouse?

    a. 15
    b. 25
    c. 35
    d. 50

147. How far in advance of a planned union picketing must a representation petition be completed?

    a. 15 days
    b. 30 days
    c. 45 days
    d. 60 days

148. According to the Labor-Management Relations Act (LMRA) of 1947, if the President steps in during a labor strike, how long of a "cooling-off" period may he require, should the strike be deemed to have national consequences?

    a. 30 days
    b. 50 days
    c. 80 days
    d. 100 days

149. The LMRA is also referred to by which of the following names?

    a. Norris-LaGuardia Act
    b. Taft-Hartley Act
    c. Wagner Act
    d. Landrum-Griffith Act

150. The Labor-Management Reporting and Disclosure Act (LMRDA) of 1959 required that *local* unions conduct leadership elections how often?

    a. Every 2 years
    b. Every 3 years
    c. Every 4 years
    d. Every 5 years

151. The Labor-Management Reporting and Disclosure Act (LMRDA) of 1959 required that *national* unions conduct leadership elections how often?

    a. Every 2 years
    b. Every 3 years
    c. Every 4 years
    d. Every 5 years

152. LMRDA is also referred to by which of the following names?

    a. Norris-LaGuardia Act
    b. Taft-Hartley Act
    c. Wagner Act
    d. Landrum-Griffith Act

153. All of the following would be legally considered unfair labor practices for an employer except

    a. Entering into positional bargaining with the employee union
    b. Entering into a hot cargo agreement with the employee union
    c. Taking disciplinary action against those who participate in unions
    d. Declining to enter into a bargain with the employee union

154. All of the following would be legally considered unfair labor practices for a union except

    a. Preventing an employee from selecting bargaining representation
    b. Requiring that employees sign a security clause to be part of the union
    c. Requiring an employee to continue in a job that is technologically obsolete
    d. Declining to enter into good faith negotiations with the employer

155. Within how many months of an incident must a labor charge be filed?

    a. 3
    b. 4
    c. 5
    d. 6

156. Before a newly forming labor union may submit a demand for recognition to the employer, what step must occur?

    a. Petition the NLRB for voluntary recognition
    b. Establish a bargaining position for the union
    c. Acquire signed authorization cards from employees
    d. Meet with the employer to discuss alternatives

157. Which of the following is defined by a union activity in which someone takes a job with a company that the union has targeted for employee unionization, and thus works to encourage employees at the new company to organize a union?

    a. Wildcatting
    b. Salting
    c. Featherbedding
    d. Leafletting

158. Which of the following is not a recognized type of picketing?

    a. Organizational
    b. Informational
    c. Petitional
    d. Recognitional

159. A labor union has recently been created at a company that manufactures heavy industrial equipment. Before negotiations can begin, the company chooses freely to acknowledge the union as the primary bargaining union for employees. In the meantime, the labor union has upcoming union elections to consider. Due to the company's decision, which of the following types of union election bars would result?

    a. Prior-petition
    b. Certification-year
    c. Voluntary-recognition
    d. Blocking-charge

160. During negotiations between an employer and the labor union, a charge of an unfair labor practice on the part of the union has arisen. The union has elections coming up soon, but the NLRA has established an election bar. Under the circumstances, which of the following types of union election bars would result?

a. Prior-petition
b. Certification-year
c. Voluntary-recognition
d. Blocking-charge

161. Which of the following types of collective bargaining positions results when the different sides agree to compromise on certain issues by taking the big picture into account?

a. Positional bargaining
b. Integrative bargaining
c. Interest-based bargaining
d. Distributive bargaining

162. Which of the following of collective bargaining results when both sides acknowledge that they have a strong motivation in the continuity of business activities, and thus proceed in negotiations with this acknowledgement?

a. Positional bargaining
b. Integrative bargaining
c. Interest-based bargaining
d. Distributive bargaining

163. *Hard bargaining* is another name for which of the following types of collective bargaining?

a. Principled bargaining
b. Coordinated bargaining
c. Integrative bargaining
d. Positional bargaining

164. *Pattern bargaining*, *whipsawing*, and *leapfrogging* are all alternate names for which of the following collective bargaining strategies?

a. Single-union bargaining
b. Multi-employer bargaining
c. Parallel bargaining
d. Multi-unit bargaining

165. Which of the following is not considered one of the criteria under which the NLRB recognizes a successor employer, or a new employer who has taken over a company?

a. Indicating a significant continuity in standard business activities
b. Establishing a clear agreement with the previous employer
c. Demonstrating a clear parallel in the products and procedures of the company
d. Assimilating all employees under the previous employer into the company

166. A review of Form(s) 5500 is a part of the due diligence process during a merger or acquisition. What does Form 5500 pertain to?

    a. Employees terminated for being in the country illegally
    b. Employees who still own stock options
    c. Employees whose wages are being garnished for child support
    d. Employee retirement plans still in force

167. A company would like to divest itself of one of its less profitable divisions. Which of the following is not a potential roadblock to doing so?

    a. A retirement plan
    b. A collective bargaining agreement
    c. Executive employment contracts
    d. A noncompete agreement

168. In which phase is it most likely that HR will first start hiring people who don't have optimal experience or qualifications and then train them for a specific job?

    a. Decline
    b. Maturity
    c. Growth
    d. Startup

169. Within how many days must an employee file a complaint with OSHA regarding retaliation from an employer for exposing a company violation?

    a. 60 days
    b. 90 days
    c. 120 days
    d. 180 days

170. Following the filing of an employee complaint, as noted in question 169, how many days does OSHA have to issue a final order?

    a. 60 days
    b. 90 days
    c. 120 days
    d. 180 days

171. If OSHA fails to issue the final order, what is the next step that the employee may take?

    a. Contact his congressional representative to discuss the matter
    b. File a law suit in a U.S. district court
    c. Request a restraining order against the employer
    d. Submit an official request that the company improve its whistleblower policy

172. In the event that a potential retaliatory action has occurred from an employer against an employee, what is generally OSHA's first goal?

    a. Have employee reinstated with full benefits and back pay
    b. File criminal charges against employer for illegal retaliation
    c. Attempt reconciliation between employer and employee
    d. Protect employee by requiring continued pay without requiring a return to work

173. Which of the following agencies is responsible for enforcing privacy laws?

    a. DOJ
    b. EEOC
    c. FTC
    d. DOL

174. The updated changes to the Equal Employment Opportunity Act of 1972 specifically included all of the following except

    a. Educational institutions
    b. Labor unions
    c. Federal government
    d. Local government

175. Compared to the total compensation package of an American employee working in the US, the total compensation package of an expatriate with similar skills and experience will be:

    a. About the same
    b. Quite a bit higher
    c. A little higher
    d. A little lower

Answer Key and Explanations

1. B: L-1. An L-1 visa allows a person already working for a US company in their home country to come to the US on a temporary basis to work for the same company here. The length of the allowed stay varies, depending on which country the person is coming from. The shortest is three months, while the longest is five years. With extensions, a person can stay in America on an L-1 visa for up to seven years.

2. D: Because the new hire will have to work with the leadership of other departments, a panel-style interview – at which the leadership of other departments is present – would be valuable in this situation. A situational interview style is useful when a candidate needs to be able to explain his decision within a hypothetical situation. That is less relevant under the circumstances described. A behavioral interview would ask the candidate how he behaved in a past situation. Again, that is not immediately relevant in this situation, nor would it be as useful as a panel interview.

3. C: In this situation, the human resources professional can assist the corporation by developing an internal test that determines the writing skills of employees. Reviewing resumes to see which writing courses recent hires have taken is largely a waste of time; the corporation already recognizes that whatever courses may have been taken did little good. Requiring that all employees take a writing course is too broad and too generic. The first step is to determine where the writing level is and to make a decision from there. Reviewing recent writing samples to see if the writing level is too low is redundant; the question indicates that the committee has already done this.

4. C: This answer choice is correct by virtue of being wrong: the Immigration Reform and Control Act does *not* require employees to favor American citizens in hiring. (In fact, this is more likely to be illegal, since the Title VII of the Civil Rights Act of 1964 makes it illegal to discriminate against someone based on national origin. That is a broad definition, but this particular activity could certainly fall within the category of Title VII prohibitions.) The Immigration Reform and Control Act does, however, afford the following: provide amnesty for all illegal immigrants that had been in the United States for at least four years, make employers responsible for providing documentation to prove the legal immigration status of their employees, and provide amnesty for agricultural workers who have worked in the United States for many years.

5. B: In this situation, the human resources professional should remain in contact with the development section of the company to ensure that the new risk management program meets all legal and procedural requirements. Answer choices A and C represent elements of this process, but neither providing the development section of the company with documentation that details current legal requirements for risk management or establishing parameters for the development section to begin assembling its new risk management program is complete in itself. Recommending a training program might be useful, but it is more likely that the development section will create its own training program that fits the unique needs of the new risk management program. In this case, once again, the human resources professional should be involved largely in an advisory position to ensure that all legal/procedural requirements are followed and met.

6. A: As with question 5, question 6 places the human resources professional in an advisory capacity. He should review any potential testing tools in advance to ensure that whatever testing program is selected meets any legal and procedural requirements that govern the company. The other answer choices contain elements of the correct answer, but none is completely correct. The human resources professional will apply company policy and legal requirements to the search for an appropriate testing program, but he may not necessarily be responsible for making the final

- 77 -

choice. The human resources professional may very well recommend that the company develop its own testing program, but this is not likely to be the first step. The recommendation for a new program will follow the determination that other programs are not suitable or appropriate.

7. A: The human resources professional is sometimes called upon to complete a cost-benefit analysis, and in this case such an analysis would be appropriate. The marketing research company needs to remain within its budget, so it is important to look at each testing option and consider what it will cost the company when compared to what it will potentially yield. Once this comparison is made, a decision can also be made. Answer choice B is an important part of the process of choosing the best testing option, but it is not necessarily a part that the human resources professional needs to complete. Any options that are already over the budget may be eliminated before they make it to the desk of the human resources professional. Answer choice C provides an option that might not really be an option—utilizing part of a testing program instead of the whole. Since there is little information within the question to justify such a decision, answer choice C has little relevance. Answer choice D offers a recommendation that is not really the human resources professional's to make; he is not in charge of the budget but rather is responsible for sticking to it and ensuring that expenses fit within the budget. More to the point, the human resources professional has been asked to make sure the testing program fits within the budget, not to find a way to *make* a testing program fit into the budget.

8. D: The NLRA specifically does not apply to agricultural workers (among other types of workers – domestic workers, contract employees, federal and state workers, etc.). There is nothing within the NLRA to prevent it from applying to administrative, corporate, or financial employees. Within each of these categories, it might be possible to find a type of worker that fits the NLRA caveat, such as a contract employee or a federal worker, but there is nothing about these other four categories that fails to fall under NLRA.

9. C: Title VII of the Civil Rights Act of 1964 made it illegal for a business to discriminate against an employee due to his national origin. The Sarbanes-Oxley Act was intended to improve accounting practices within public companies. The Rehabilitation Act penalized businesses for discriminating against employees who have a disability. HIPAA, the Health Insurance Portability and Accountability Act of 1996, in part, protects workers against losing their health coverage immediately if they lose their jobs.

10. D: HIPAA, the Health Insurance Portability and Accountability Act of 1996, in part, protects workers against losing their health coverage immediately if they lose their jobs. The Sarbanes-Oxley Act was intended to improve accounting practices within public companies. The Rehabilitation Act penalized businesses for discriminating against employees who have a disability. Title VII of the Civil Rights Act of 1964 made it illegal for a business to discriminate against an employee due to his national origin.

11. C: A brown-bag meeting is considered more of a bottom-up form of communication: at a brown bag meeting, employees are invited to take part in the discussion and share their ideas. Top-down communication would focus more on the management informing employees of decisions. As a result, the other answer choices reflect more of top-down communication: posters, bulletin board postings, and newsletters.

12. D: In some cases, the human resources professional might be asked to track changes in employee pay. For the most part, however, employee raises will not be an expense item that is under the human resources professional's control. The other options – supplies, travel, and

- 78 -

maintenance – represent standard expense items that the human resources professional tracks and controls.

13. B: Athlete or entertainer visas fall under the "P" category (P-1, P-2, P-3, and P-4). The "R" category of visas is for those performing religious work (R-1). The "H" category of visas is for temporary workers of all varieties (H-1B, H-1C, H-2A, H-2B, H-3). The "L" category of workers is for those being transferred to a new position within the same company (L-1A, L-1B, L-2).

14. C: In the SMART model, the letter "R" stands for Realistic. The other options (Reasonable, Reversible, and Representative) do not fit into the SMART model, which is designed to assist a company in defining its long-term goals for development.

15. A: While polygraph testing might have the goal of "justice" in mind, it actually falls under the Department of Labor. The Federal Trade Commission governs fair credit reviews, while the USCIS (or the United States Citizenship and Immigration Services) governs immigration laws. For employers, the Department of Justice is involved in privacy laws that apply to employees.

16. D: *Risk* is defined as Probability x Consequences. In other words, a business must multiply the odds of something occurring by the results of that occurrence. The occurrence itself is a part of the process that leads to consequences, but it is not a direct element within the standard risk formula. The result of this formula enables a business to employ prevention or avoidance options.

17. B: Employment practices liability insurance is available to provide businesses with a form of *risk transfer*; with the insurance, the business can transfer at least part of the cost of risk to another source. Reviewing employment policies to avoid the chances of an employee lawsuit is considered *risk mitigation*. Taking advance action to consider potentials for risk and prevent problems from occurring is part of *risk avoidance*. Being familiar with chances of risk and creating a financial buffer against future costs is considered *risk acceptance*.

18. C: A second IRCA (Immigration Reform and Control Act) violation results in a penalty of not less than $2,000 and not more than $5,000 for each unauthorized employee. The first violation results in a penalty of not less than $250 and not more than $2,000 for each unauthorized employee. A third violation results in a penalty of not less than $5,000 and not more than $10,000 for each unauthorized employee. Note that answer choices A and B combine penalty information for the first violation but are not penalties in their own right.

19. C: The best way for Gina to handle this situation is to be honest and share with her employees as many facts as possible. Having Gina write notes to all employees might be a kind gesture, but it is but one step that she can take and hardly encompasses a full approach in this situation. Similarly, Silvia might recommend that Gina petition the call center to retain the department, but the move might also be entirely fruitless if the decision is made. (At this point, Gina's best option is to keep the lines of communication open with employees, rather than offering them false hopes.) And while Gina might decide to help the employees find new jobs, this is not part of her job description, nor should this be a primary recommendation. What is more, Gina would have to do this on her own time, as it would be unwise for Silvia to recommend that Gina take company time to relocate her employees to other jobs, regardless of the impending lay-offs.

20. A: If the candidate mentions family, an appropriate question, particularly for a company that has locations around the world, would be to ask if the candidate is willing to relocate. The other questions are inappropriate (Do you and your wife plan to have children? Do any other family members live with you? Does your wife also work?); the only way to acquire this information would be if the candidate decides to volunteer it.

21. D: Title VII of the Civil Rights Act of 1964 covers the following types of document retention: apprentice selection records, employee resumes, and tax deductions. It does not, however, apply to a business's affirmative action plan, which falls under Executive Order 11246.

22. A: Construct validity is the measurement of the relationship between the characteristics of each employee and his actual performance in the position. Criterion validity results when a certain criterion (or work trait) is predicted and then results. Concurrent validity is a type of criterion validity (along with predictive validity). Content validity is simply a test that measures whether or not a candidate is qualified to complete an important part of the job. A simple example might be an audition for a dance company; the job description requires the dancers to perform in the company, so the construct validity starts by measuring whether or not those at the audition have acceptable dance training.

23. B: Cultural noise is a type of bias in which the candidate begins responding as he believes the interviewer would prefer. For instance, for a job that requires extensive travel, a candidate might attempt to sway the odds in his favor by claiming to enjoy travel, even if he has no travel experience in other jobs (and/or might not really care to travel but hopes to get the job). The halo effect results from an interviewer focusing on a single good quality to define the candidate. The horn effect is the opposite of this; it occurs when the interviewer focuses on a single negative quality, over all other qualities, to rate the candidate. The central tendency occurs if an interviewer is unable to make a clear decision about a preferred candidate and averages their results.

24. B: Bottom-up methods of communication include an open-door policy, webcasts, and staff meetings; in each case, the employees are considered an active part of the discussion and even decision making. Individual letters represent a top-down method of communication, because top-down communication focuses more on the management informing employees of decisions.

25. B: According to FLSA, work schedule documents should be retained for a minimum of 2 years. Job announcement should be retained for at least 1 year. Employee contracts should be retained for at least 3 years. FLSA does not have a minimum retention rate of 5 years for any documents, although businesses may choose to extend the minimum retention to 5 years for certain documents to ensure they maintain certain records.

26. D: Medical workers are not identified as a separate category under the EEO-1 report. Sales workers, service workers, and craft workers, however, all represent separate EEO-1 categories.

27. B: A short-form application is appropriate for job transfers and job promotions within the same company, so this would be appropriate for Michal's situation. A job-specific application is useful for companies that hire a number of workers for the same type of (or similar) jobs. A long-form application is considered standard for allowing candidates to include their entire educational and work history. A weighted application is appropriate for companies that need to focus on certain candidate qualifications over others.

28. D: A nondirective interview style occurs when the interviewer asks broad questions to allow the candidate to answer candidly and comfortably. A behavioral interview would ask the candidate how he behaved in a past situation, with the intent being to use past experience to anticipate future actions. A patterned interview focuses on a group of questions that apply specifically to the job and what will be required in that position. A directive interview is highly focused and organized, with the interviewer asking the same questions of all candidates.

29. B: The WARN Act of 1988 requires that the plant inform employees at least 60 days in advance of the impending lay-offs. The other options – 30 days, 90 days, or 120 days – are either too short or

are unnecessarily early. (The plant might not know 120 days in advance, so it would be difficult to inform employees this long before the event.)

30. C: Turnover analysis results from dividing the average number of employees over a given time frame by the number of employees who left the business. Accession rate is something of the reverse of this: the number of new hires when compared to the full number of employees in a business. The replacement cost shows businesses how much cost goes into hiring new employees; these costs might include overtime costs and training costs. The quality of hire is determined when a business establishes an example of a quality hire and then compares other employees or new hires against it.

31. D: A histogram is useful for reviewing a series of random events to locate a potential pattern within them. A check sheet is equivalent to a checklist of expected results; the human resources professional would then compare results to the check sheet and check off what has occurred. A pareto chart measures two types of data; the information can yield results about the most important factor among many factors. A scatter chart also measures two types of data on an *xy* graph.

32. A: The "I" in the Six Sigma DMAIC philosophy stands for Improve, instead of Identify. Control, Define, and Measure are all part of the philosophy (along with Analyze).

33. C: The best practice retention period for employee records that relate to discrimination charges is 7 years after the employee leaves the company. This is defined by the Rehabilitation Act of 1973. The purpose is to maintain necessary records in case the employee pursues legal action. A retention period of 2 years or 5 years is too short. The business many prefer to retain such records for 10 years, but the Rehabilitation Act of 1973 identifies 7 years as "best practice."

34. B: The Psychomotor Assessment Test is useful for measuring a candidate's motor skills in completing certain tasks. A short order cook would need to be able to prepare food quickly and efficiently, so such a test would be appropriate in this case. A Cognitive Ability Test focuses more on a candidate's problem-solving and analytical skills. A Physical Assessment Test measures whether or not a candidate is physically able to handle certain tasks. (For example, working for a delivery company might require the physical ability to lift and carry heavy objects; a Physical Assessment Test would be appropriate in such a situation.) An Aptitude Test measures basic skills such as typing, reading, or calculating simple math problems.

35. B: The Walsh Healy Public Contracts Act of 1936 determines that for any government contract over $10,000 the local minimum wage requirement applies to workers. The other answer choice options ($5,000; $15,000; and $20,000) are either too low or already fall within the minimum requirement of $10,000.

36. A: The Walsh Healy Public Contracts Act of 1936 applies to all types of government contract work except construction work. There is nothing in the act to prevent it from applying to technology, security, or delivery work in government contracts.

37. A: It takes only one complaint about a potential FLSA violation for a government audit to occur. As a result, businesses are expected to take FLSA rules seriously, and the human resources professional must be very familiar with the rules to avoid even an unintentional violation. The other answer choices (2, 3, and 5) are all too high. By the time that many complaints arise, the audit will already be in progress or have been completed.

38. C: FMLA rules allow an employee to take off time to care for a family member within one of the following categories: spouse, child, or parent. In some cases, an extended family member may

apply, if the individual can prove a close relationship with that family member. ("Distant uncle rarely seen" does not apply.) Additionally, a romantic partner does not apply; FMLA rules make it clear that the person must be recognized as a spouse within his or her state. FMLA rules do apply, however, to an individual who needs to rest during a difficult pregnancy, care for a newborn infant, or adopt or foster a child.

39. D: Department of Labor form WH-385 is appropriate for FMLA regulations that apply to caring for a covered service member. Form WH-380-E applies to employees facing serious health conditions. Form WH-380-F applies to employees who are caring for family members with serious health conditions. Form WH-384 applies to exigency leave for family of military service members.

40. C: The steps in the mediation process include the following: Structure, Introductions, Fact-finding, Options, and Negotiating. "Opinions" is not one of these steps. (In fact, it is likely due to opinions that the mediation was necessary in the first place.)

41. D: An employee-absenteeism policy might include information about *when* a doctor's note is required, but it does not necessarily need to require a doctor's note in all situations. This might prove to be onerous to employees who are genuinely ill at home for a day but are not ill enough to visit a doctor. Additionally, a requirement for a note for *each* sick day absence would be an inappropriate policy, as the employee might be out for 4-5 days but is not likely to see the doctor each of those days. A good policy should, however, include the following: a statement about how many sick days each employee receives, an indication of how sick days are counted within the calendar, and information about how each absence is counted in days.

42. A: Governmental barriers were identified as part of the need for the Glass Ceiling Act of 1991. Recruitment and corporate barriers fall under the category of internal structural barriers; educational barriers fall under the category of societal barriers.

43. D: The acronym BFOQ stands for *bona fide occupational qualification* and describes an exception to any of the anti-discrimination laws for employment. (For instance, in some religious organizations, only men may be ordained as ministers/priests. This would be considered a bona fide occupational qualification.) The other acronyms do not reflect any recognized terms and certainly have no connection to exceptions within the anti-discrimination laws.

44. B: The Latin phrase *respondeat superior* translates to mean "let the master answer" and suggests that companies have a measure of responsibility for employee actions, if employee actions result from job responsibilities. The phrase "friend of the court" comes from the Latin *amicus curiae*. The phrase "with connected strength" comes from the Latin *coniunctis viribus*. The phrase "thrown to the lions" comes from the Latin *damnatio ad bestias*.

45. B: According to FLSA, children must be at least 16 years of age to be hired for non-farm jobs. Children cannot be hired for such jobs at the age of 15, and the ages of 18 and 19 no longer apply to children.

46. B: A drug screening test can be required of any candidate for a job, and the medical examination conditions of ADA do not prevent a candidate from being tested for drug use, regardless of disability. Polygraph tests, driving tests, and aptitude tests are not part of potential medical examinations, and all of these tests must be administered with certain stipulations from ADA.

47. D: The Privacy Act of 1974 reflects data collection activities within federal agencies. It does not apply to private employers. The Fair Credit Reporting Act of 1970, the Immigration and Nationality

Act of 1952, and the Civil Rights Act of 1991 all currently have elements that apply to private employers.

48. C: Reengineering is defined as an attempt to improve overall business operations so that customers benefit from the process. Workforce expansion, as the name indicates, is an increase in employees for a business to reach certain goals. Divestiture is a business decision to eliminate a department by laying off employees or moving them to another department. Offshoring, or outsourcing, refers to a business's decision to move certain activities to another location (usually international) to reduce costs.

49. B: Divestiture is defined as a business decision to eliminate a department by laying off employees or moving them to another department. Reengineering is an attempt to improve overall business operations so that customers benefit from the process. Workforce expansion, as the name indicates, is an increase in employees for a business to reach certain goals. Offshoring, or outsourcing, refers to a business's decision to move certain activities to another location (usually international) to reduce costs.

50. D: The categories for EEO-1 do not include an option for European. They do, however, include the categories Native Hawaiian, Alaska Native, and Asian.

51. D: All of the above. Companies of all sizes have offshored many functions and processes, including accounting, payroll, and call centers. Some companies use offshore firms for many of their HR functions.

52. D: The EEO-1 report must be completed on or before September 30 of each year (as this reflects the federal fiscal calendar). The other dates – January 31, April 1, and June 15 – all reflect possible times for submitting the report, if viewed as falling "before" September 30, but they do not reflect the required date. Also, it is unlikely that any human resources professional would submit the report on these dates. It is far more likely that the report will be completed and submitted closer to the required date.

53. C: Private employers with 100 employees or more – except for those within excluded categories – must complete the EEO-1 report. The other answer choices are either too low (50 and 75) or too high (200). In the case of answer choice D, this number of employees falls well within the required reporting, but it does not reflect the *minimum* stated by law.

54. C: Private employers within all forms of major educational institutions (primary, secondary, and post-secondary) are excluded from having to complete EEO-1 filings. Private employers who fall within the areas of administration, banking, or construction, and have 100 employees or more, must complete the report.

55. A: A PPO, or Preferred Provider Organization, plan does not require that patients first contact a "gatekeeper" for medical treatment but allows patients to choose from a broad network. A POS, or Point of Service, plan offers a network (like a PPO) but allows patients to meet with a physician outside this network and request reimbursement later on. An HMO, or Health Maintenance Organization, plan does require a "gatekeeper" but also focuses on lower health care costs for patients and care that aims to prevent higher costs later on. An FFS, or Fee-for-service, plan is generally the most costly for patients but allows them to make their own selection of facilities and physicians.

56. C: An HMO, or Health Maintenance Organization, plan does require a "gatekeeper" but also focuses on lower health care costs for patients and care that aims to prevent higher costs later on. A

PPO, or Preferred Provider Organization, plan does not require that patients first contact a "gatekeeper" for medical treatment but allows patients to choose from a broad network. A POS, or Point of Service, plan offers a network (like a PPO) but allows patients to meet with a physician outside this network and request reimbursement later on. An FFS, or Fee-for-service, plan is generally the most costly for patients but allows them to make their own selection of facilities and physicians.

57. D: An FFS, or Fee-for-service, plan is generally the most costly for patients but allows them to make their own selection of facilities and physicians. A PPO, or Preferred Provider Organization, plan does not require that patients first contact a "gatekeeper" for medical treatment but allows patients to choose from a broad network. A POS, or Point of Service, plan offers a network (like a PPO) but allows patients to meet with a physician outside this network and request reimbursement later on. An HMO, or Health Maintenance Organization, plan does require a "gatekeeper" but also focuses on lower health care costs for patients and care that aims to prevent higher costs later on.

58. C: Medicare is not a voluntary benefit; in other words, employers must provide it. Short-term disability insurance, vision insurance, and life insurance are all considered voluntary benefits that the employer may choose, or not choose, to offer.

59. A: Social security, like Medicare, is an involuntary benefit that employers must provide. Vacation time, qualified pension plans, and paid holidays, on the other hand, are all voluntary benefits that employers have the option to provide or not provide for employees.

60. A: To cut costs. Cost reduction is by far the biggest reason companies turn to offshoring. Labor costs in most of the world are far lower than they are here, and in many places, there is an abundance of skilled workers who can perform the jobs for far less than American workers.

61. D: The ECPA, or Electronic Communications Privacy Act of 1986, governs an employer's ability to monitor the electronic communication of employees. FLSA is the Fair Labor Standards Act of 1938 that covers a number of employer requirements but does not refer specifically to employers monitoring employee electronic communications. (This is hardly surprising, as electronic communications would have been limited when the legislation was enacted.) OSHA, the Occupational Safety and Health Administration, is a department instead of a piece of legislation. (There is an OSHA Act, but it goes by this name, while OSHA is recognized specifically as the department.) MSHA refers to the Mine Safety and Health Act of 1977 that applies to mine workers.

62. A: The Motivation/Hygiene Theory of 1959, which focuses on raising the value of a job in the eyes of the employee, is attributed to Fredrick Herzberg. Clayton Alderfer is responsible for the ERG Theory of 1969; Victor Vroom is credited with the Expectancy Theory of 1964; Abraham Maslow is credited with the Hierarchy of Needs Theory of 1954.

63. B: The ERG Theory of 1969, which looks at the levels Existence, Relatedness, and Growth among employees, is attributed to Clayton Alderfer. Fredrick Herzberg is credited with the Motivation/Hygiene Theory of 1959; Victor Vroom is credited with the Expectancy Theory of 1964; Abraham Maslow is credited with the Hierarchy of Needs Theory of 1954.

64. D: The Expectancy Theory of 1964, which considers employee motivation in view of the potential for reward, is attributed to Victor Vroom. Fredrick Herzberg is credited with the Motivation/Hygiene Theory of 1959; Clayton Alderfer is responsible for the ERG Theory of 1969; Abraham Maslow is credited with the Hierarchy of Needs Theory of 1954.

65. C: The Hierarchy of Needs Theory of 1954, which discusses the relationship between an employee and his job and which is also the starting point for many of the other theorists, is attributed to Abraham Maslow. Fredrick Herzberg is credited with the Motivation/Hygiene Theory of 1959; Clayton Alderfer is responsible for the ERG Theory of 1969; Victor Vroom is credited with the Expectancy Theory of 1964.

66. C: The fourth of B.F. Skinner's strategies is Extinction. The other answer choices – Termination, Encouragement, and Actualization – are not specific strategies laid out by Skinner but rather might fall under the four he did describe.

67. D: Negative Reinforcement occurs when a good behavior occurs and a negative result for behavior is removed. The behavioral review would be considered a negative result of poor behavior; when this is removed after a week of no employee complains, Kathryn is applying Negative Reinforcement. Answer choices A reflects Skinner's strategy of Punishment. Answer choice C reflects Skinner's strategy of Positive Reinforcement. Answer choice B reflects a possible combination of Positive Reinforcement and Extinction. It does not, however, represent a single strategy laid out by Skinner.

68. A: The fourth leadership style as presented in the Hersey-Blanchard theory is Participating. Directing and Guiding fall under the leadership style Telling; Motivating falls under the leadership style Selling.

69. A: Transactional leadership occurs when a leader offers some form of a transaction as the result of meeting a goal; in other words the manager is utilizing transactional leadership by offering a reward if employees complete certain monthly goals. Answer choice B reflects a coaching style of leadership. Answer choice C reflects more of a directive style of leadership. Answer choice D reflects a *laissez-faire* style of leadership.

70. C: The widespread nature of the company locations means that a questionnaire is going to be the most effective way to acquire feedback; the questionnaire can be sent out, and employees can then complete it and return it by a certain time. A focus group is impractical, as it might be difficult to get enough people together for the discussion. Interviews and observation can prove to be cumbersome, both to employees and management, because they might require extensive travel and/or arranging of schedules.

71. B: The fourth element in SWOT is Threats. In other words, SWOT as an environmental scanning tool requires a review of Strengths, Weaknesses, Opportunities, and Threats. The other answer choices (Tools, Targets, and Techniques) are not a part of this particular environmental scanning tool.

72. D: With both employees having similar skills and looking for reduced hours, job-sharing might be the best option both for them and the company. Having the employees on-call might be useful for reduced hours, but without more information on the type of business it might also be difficult to arrange. (On-call work, for instance, would be of little use in a standard office environment and might do more to disrupt activities.) Telecommuting is useful for cost reduction, but it does not necessarily address the specific needs of this situation. An internship makes little sense as both employees are already full employees instead of students looking to acquire experience.

73. B: The Equal Pay Act, created in 1963, forbids any type of discrimination based on the employee's gender. The Portal to Portal Act of 1947, determined that employers cannot be required to compensate employees who commute long distances to work. The Davis Beacon Act was created

in 1931, and the National Labor Relations Act was created in 1935; both fall before the legislation of the Fair Labor Standards Act of 1938, so both are irrelevant.

74. A: The Portal to Portal Act, created in 1947, determined that employers cannot be required to compensate employees who commute long distances to work. The Equal Pay Act of 1963 forbids any type of discrimination based on the employee's gender. The Davis Beacon Act was created in 1931, and the National Labor Relations Act was created in 1935; both fall before the legislation of the Fair Labor Standards Act of 1938, so both are irrelevant.

75. C: The Sherman Anti-Trust Act was created in 1890 and represents the first piece of legislation to affect the movement for labor rights within the United States. The Clayton Act followed in 1914, the Railway Labor Act in 1926, and the Norris-La Guardia Act in 1932.

76. A: The SEC is responsible for enforcing corporate governance. The EEOC and the OFCCP enforce civil rights laws. MSHA is the Mine Safety and Health Act of 1977, so it is not an enforcing agency. This particular piece of legislation focuses on the specific requirements for mine workers and does not enforce corporate governance in general.

77. D: The Drug-Free Workplace Act of 1988 applies to federal contracts of a minimum of $100,000. All other answer choices ($50,000; $75,000; $80,000) are too low to fall under the requirements of this piece of legislation.

78. C: Any penalties for failing to comply with the Drug-Free Workplace Act (1988) must fall in line with standards that were laid out in the Rehabilitation Act, which was passed in 1973. The Davis Beacon Act of 1931 placed federal regulations on minimum wage. The Fair Labor Standards Act of 1938 also focused on compensation rights for workers. Similarly, the Service Contract Act of 1965 focused on compensation for federal contract workers.

79. A: While education about workplace safety is implied, it is not one of the three primary expectations of OSHA. These expectations are as follows: provide employees a safe place to work; ensure that federal safety standards are met; ensure that occupational safety standards are met.

80. B: An "other-than-serious" violation has a maximum fine of $7,000. (In this case, "other-than-serious" refers to some form of a hazard that would not necessarily result in death or severe physical danger.) A $5,000 fine usually falls under the category of "willful." There is no stated OSHA fine of either $10,000 or $12,000. It is, of course, possible for OSHA to assign such a fine to a business, but this fine exceeds the "other-than-serious" category and would likely be the result of a different type of violation.

81. C: A repeat violation can result in a fine as high as $70,000. (OSHA does not necessarily assign a penalty this high, but it has the right to do so, if a violation occurs more than once.) The amounts $25,000 and $40,000 would fall under this category, but they do not represent the maximum that OSHA can fine for a repeat violation. A fine of $85,000 would only result from multiple violations and does not represent a single violation.

82. B: Employers with at least 11 employees are required to complete OSHA forms. A business with only 4 employees does not have to complete the forms (although this might be recommended). Businesses with 14 or 17 employees fall well within the OSHA requirements.

83. B: OSHA Form 300A is intended to be a Summary of Work-Related Injuries and Illnesses. OSHA Form 300 is intended to be a Log of Work-Related Injuries and Illnesses. OSHA Form 301 is intended to be an Injury and Illness Incident Report. OSHA Form 301A does not exist.

84. C: OSHA Form 301 is intended to be an Injury and Illness Incident Report. OSHA Form 300 is intended to be a Log of Work-Related Injuries and Illnesses. OSHA Form 300A is intended to be a Summary of Work-Related Injuries and Illnesses. OSHA Form 301A does not exist.

85. A: OSHA Form 300 is intended to be a Log of Work-Related Injuries and Illnesses. OSHA Form 300A is intended to be a Summary of Work-Related Injuries and Illnesses. OSHA Form 301 is intended to be an Injury and Illness Incident Report. OSHA Form 301A does not exist.

86. C: Federal recommendations state that employers should retain OSHA forms for a minimum of 5 years. Retaining forms for 2 or 3 years is too brief. Forms may certainly be retained for 7 years, but this exceeds the minimum federal recommendations.

87. A: Given the sensitive nature of the disease, the contraction of hepatitis, even in the workplace, would be grounds for the employer to use a case number instead of the employee's name. Unless an employee specifically requests a case number, there is no need to assign one to a case file in any of the following situations: an employee contracts the flu after receiving a flu vaccine in the workplace, an employee develops food poisoning in the workplace, or an employee receives a head injury in the workplace.

88. C: During a CSHO inspection, the following should occur: the CSHO should present his credentials, the CSHO should hold an opening conference, the CSHO should tour the facilities, and the CSHO should hold a closing conference. It cannot be expected that the problem, if one is determined to be present, will be resolved during the inspection. A resolution is usually a follow-up result of the inspection.

89. B: Should an employer receive a citation, he has a maximum of 15 days to file a Notice of Contest. The employer may certainly file the Notice of Contest within 7 days, but there is still time beyond this to consider the decision. Filing a Notice of Contest 30 or 45 days after receiving the citation would be too late.

90. A: NIOSH created the HHE, or Health Hazard Evaluation, to assist in responding to employer, as well as employee, concerns about workplace hazards. A VPP is a Voluntary Protection Program in which employers may voluntarily choose to participate. (The standards for safety are significantly stricter.) MSH refers to Mine Safety and Health and usually applies to the legislation that passed in 1977. MSD refers to musculoskeletal disorders that result from poor ergonomics in the workplace.

91. C: Poor ergonomics result in the largest number of work-related injuries and health problems in the United States each year. Job-related stress and psychological strain no doubt contribute to a number of problems as well, but these areas are much more difficult to quantify. Excess physical output would apply largely to jobs with high physical activity – which is not necessarily a high percentage of jobs in the United States – whereas poor ergonomics can affect employees in almost every job.

92. B: OSHA's requirements apply almost universally to businesses with at least 11 employees. (A business with 10 or fewer employees is not expected to complete OSHA forms or even assemble an Injury and Illness Prevention Plan.) Businesses with 15 or 17 employees certainly fall within OSHA's regulations.

93. D: NLRA, or the National Labor Relations Act of 1935, applies primarily to labor standards in the United States, as well as the relationship between employers and their workers. FECA refers to the Federal Employees Compensation Act of 1916; BLBA refers to the Black Lung Benefits Act of 1969/1977; LHWCA refers to the Longshore and Harbor Workers' Compensation Act of 1927.

94. B: A promissory estoppel is defined as an occasion when an employer offers an employee some form of reward for completing an action, and then fails to follow through with that reward. Fraudulent misrepresentation is similar but is defined more broadly as any sort of promise made to a candidate to persuade him to take a position with the company (followed by a failure to act on this promise). Constructive discharge is defined as an employee's decision to quit when an employer creates hostile working conditions. Duty of good faith is simply a tradition of common law by which those who work together are expected to behave in all fairness and honesty toward one another.

95. D: A suggestion box offers employees a measure of anonymity in proffering ideas to the company's upper management. Brown bag lunches and focus groups require employees to participate actively, and as the scenario indicates many employees would be uncomfortable with this. Email might be private, but it certainly is not anonymous, so it would not represent the best recommendation for Helena to make.

96. B: BARS refers to the Behaviorally Anchored Rating Scale that employers may use internally to determine whether employee behavior is meeting the standards. MBO (with no "S" at the end) typically refers to Management by Objective, in which businesses set certain goals and work toward reaching them within an established frame of time. TQM (no "S" at the end) refers to Total Quality Management, which is a program designed to improve business activity to increase the value for customers. PBT (also with no "S" at the end) refers to Performance-Based Training and is intended to assist employees with improving their performance in certain jobs.

97. D: Managers are encouraged to give employees about one week advance notice for a scheduled performance evaluation. Five days might be good, but a full week is better and avoids "springing it" on the employee. Giving the employee 2 days or 3 days is far too short.

98. B: A forced distribution usually results in rating employees along a bell curve. In a paired comparison, each employee's performance viewed in the context of another employee's performance. A ranking system is usually better for a smaller group of employees but can be difficult to organize with a larger group. A nominal scale is not recognized as a type of employee rating system.

99. C: A ranking system is usually better for a smaller group of employees but can be difficult to organize with a larger group. In a paired comparison, each employee's performance viewed in the context of another employee's performance. A forced distribution usually results in rating employees along a bell curve. A nominal scale is not recognized as a type of employee rating system.

100. A: In a paired comparison, each employee's performance viewed in the context of another employee's performance. A forced distribution usually results in rating employees along a bell curve. A ranking system is usually better for a smaller group of employees but can be difficult to organize with a larger group. A nominal scale is not recognized as a type of employee rating system.

101. C: Banquet-style seating, in which groups of employees will be arranged at tables, is best for a training session with small group activities. Classroom-style seating is best if the employees will simply be facing the front of a room and listening to a speaker. Chevron-style seating is best for a combination of activities that include video presentations and group interaction. Theater-style seating accommodates the largest number of people and also works well for various presentations.

102. B: Chevron-style seating is best for a combination of activities that include video presentations and group interaction. Classroom-style seating is best if the employees will simply be facing the front of a room and listening to a speaker. Banquet-style seating, in which groups of employees will

be arranged at tables, is best for a training session with small group activities. Theater-style seating accommodates the largest number of people and also works well for various presentations.

103. D: Theater-style seating accommodates the largest number of people and also works well for various presentations. Classroom-style seating is best if the employees will simply be facing the front of a room and listening to a speaker. Chevron-style seating is best for a combination of activities that include video presentations and group interaction. Banquet-style seating, in which groups of employees will be arranged at tables, is best for a training session with small group activities.

104. A: Philip B. Crosby is responsible for the term *zero defects*, as it relates to an ideal performance standard for businesses. W. Edwards Deming began the quality movement (of the 1940s) by focusing on the consumer for improving business standards. Joseph M. Juran followed Deming with a similar focus on quality. Dr. Kaoru Ishikawa is credited with applying data analysis tools to company activities with the goal of quality improvement.

105. D: The change process theory includes three stages: Unfreezing, Moving, and Refreezing. Implementing is not one of the stages within the change process theory.

106. D: Fair use includes the following scenarios: use of material for educational purposes, limited copying of material (i.e., 10 or fewer copies for a limited number of individuals), and use of a single paragraph from a book (i.e., small percentage of total). Using quoted information—that is, information from another source—within a company motto is definitely *not* considered fair use; as the company motto represents the company and, in this sense, applies to its larger goal of making a profit, the use of the quoted material would be considered a copyright violation.

107. C: The Immigration Act of 1990 limited the number of temporary workers applying under H-1B status to 65,000 each year. This number includes answer choices A and B (45,000 and 50,000, respectively), but both of these amounts fall under the stated maximum. Answer choice D (70,000) is too high.

108. C: The updated law HR 4306, which was passed in 2005, now allows for I-9 forms to be stored electronically, such as in PDF. Prior to this, the forms were only allowed to be stored in the media paper, microfilm, or microfiche.

109. B: A business must complete the I-9 form for new employees within 3 days of employment. The business may certainly complete the form within 1 day, but this is not the stated maximum. Completing the forms after 3 days (i.e., 5 days or 7 days) violates the law.

110. A: The Immigration Reform and Control Act (IRCA) of 1986 applies to businesses with minimum of 4 employees. The other answer choices – 7, 10, and 12 – are too high. IRCA regulations apply to very small businesses.

111. B: Line of sight is defined as the knowledge employees have about how their work behavior affects their compensation. An entitlement philosophy provides greater compensation for employees with more seniority. A total rewards strategy reviews a business's resources for bringing in, and retaining, certain employees. Organizational culture is the larger category of which line of sight and entitlement philosophy are a part; organizational culture is simply the overall "culture" of a business and its relationship between management and employees.

112. D: Exemptions are specific, and in this case only answer choice D reflects a legitimate exemption status: due to the nature of the job, and the fact that the police department only has four

members, these officers would be exempt from overtime requirements. The high school coach would not necessarily be exempt from overtime requirements, just because he has to take students to games. The large farm that employs teenagers during the summer would definitely *not* be exempt from child labor requirements. And the firefighters might be exempt from overtime requirements – under certain circumstances (which do not appear to be present in this situation) – but they are certainly not exempt from minimum wage requirements.

113. C: The exemption status for the first (or last) week of employment only applies if the employee works less than the full week. As the employee is working the full week during the first week of employment, no exemption status is appropriate. The other answer choices—unpaid leave under FMLA, suspensions for inappropriate workplace behavior, and offsetting military pay—are all eligible for exemptions.

114. A: A hostile takeover of your company. He is most likely preparing to launch a hostile takeover attempt. He doesn't need to own a large amount of company stock in order to ask the SEC to investigate the company, and short selling involves selling stock, not buying it. A friendly acquisition usually begins with talks between the two parties, not massive stock buys.

115. B: Children as young as 14 may work, according to FLSA, but there are conditions that apply to hiring children this age. Children of 13 may not be legally hired by most businesses. Children of 15 and 16 are beyond the minimum age.

116. A: Children as young as 14 may work in retail, as well as technical and administrative positions (assuming the children in question have the skills/knowledge for such jobs). They may not, however, work in farm jobs; these are reserved for children of at least 16.

117. C: Reporting pay is defined as pay legally required whether or not an employer has immediate work available for an employee. Geographic pay is simply the pay scale that applies to employees in different geographic locations (ensuring that they receive a similar ratio of compensation, regardless of location). On-call pay is defined as pay provided for employees who respond to a work situation at short notice. Call-back pay is defined as pay provided for employees who must come into work beyond the scheduled work hours.

118. B: On-call pay is defined as pay provided for employees who respond to a work situation at short notice. Geographic pay is simply the pay scale that applies to employees in different geographic locations (ensuring that they receive a similar ratio of compensation, regardless of location). Reporting pay is defined as pay legally required whether or not an employer has immediate work available for an employee. Call-back pay is defined as pay provided for employees who must come into work beyond the scheduled work hours.

119. D: Call-back pay is defined as pay provided for employees who must come into work beyond the scheduled work hours. Geographic pay is simply the pay scale that applies to employees in different geographic locations (ensuring that they receive a similar ratio of compensation, regardless of location). Reporting pay is defined as pay legally required whether or not an employer has immediate work available for an employee. On-call pay is defined as pay provided for employees who respond to a work situation at short notice.

120. C: Knowledge, accountability, and problem solving are part of the HAY system. Review is not considered a part of this system, although it might, by default, fall under one of the other categories.

121. A: Wage compression is defined as an increased rate of pay for a new employee, due to that employee's education or experience. Compa-ration is defined as a method for an employer to judge

how an employee's pay compares to the standard average. Range placement is simply the overall placement of an employee's pay within a set range; pay structure refers to a company's overall system for establishing compensation.

122. C: Accordingly to FMLA rules, the established radius for employees in private businesses (as opposed to state or federal agencies) is 75 miles. The radius of 30 or 50 miles is too small. The radius of 85 miles exceeds the FMLA standard.

123. D: FMLA applies to private employers with a minimum of 50 employees. The other answer choices – 15, 20, and 35 – are too low for the FMLA minimum.

124. B: Form WH-381 is identified as the "eligibility, rights, and responsibilities notice" for employees regarding FMLA. Form WH-382 is identified as a "designation notice" to inform employees about FMLA requirements for factors such as a required medical certification or a required fitness-for-duty certification. The other answer choices do not reflect significant FMLA forms.

125. C: Form WH-382 is identified as a "designation notice" to inform employees about FMLA requirements for factors such as a required medical certification or a required fitness-for-duty certification. Form WH-381 is identified as the "eligibility, rights, and responsibilities notice" for employees regarding FMLA. The other answer choices do not reflect significant FMLA forms.

126. B: If the leave is considered foreseeable, the employee is expected to notify his employer at least 30 days in advance. An advance notice of 15 days is too short, while an advance notice of 45 or 60 days is not required (though certainly not inappropriate, if the employee expects the leave to be necessary that far in advance).

127. B: If the leave is foreseeable but the employee fails to provide his employer with appropriate advance notice, the employer may delay FMLA coverage for 30 days. The employer may, of course, delay coverage for less than 30 days—so 15 days is an option—but the employer has a full 30 days. The employer may not, however, delay coverage beyond this, so 45 days or 60 days is far too long.

128. C: FMLA leave falls into one of the following three categories: continuous, reduced, or intermittent. FMLA does not provide for permanent leave, in the sense that the employer is not expected to provide coverage if the employee ceases to be part of the company. Permanent leave is ultimately termination and falls under different laws altogether.

129. D: The human resources professional is not expected to avoid simultaneous leave within the company. This may be inevitable, and the company cannot block employees from taking approved FMLA leave. The human resources professional is, however, expected to be familiar with FMLA requirements and changes, to educate management about FMLA rules, and to develop an FMLA documentation policy for the company.

130. D: VEVRA is the Vietnam Era Veterans' Readjustment Act and does not play a role in regulating voluntary benefits programs. The other answer choices – ERISA (Employee Retirement Income Security Act), HIPAA (Health Insurance Portability and Accountability Act), and COBRA (Consolidated Omnibus Budget Reconciliation Act) – are all related to regulating voluntary benefits programs.

131. C: In graded vesting, at least 20% must be vested after three years of employment. Vesting 10% or 15% is too low. Vesting 25% is acceptable, but it does not reflect the minimum requirement for graded vesting.

132. D: In cliff vesting, 100% must be vested after five years of employment. The other answer choices—two years, three years, and four years—are too low. It is certainly acceptable to vest 100% after these amounts of time, but the full five years are provided for this.

133. B: High context culture. In high context cultures, people tend not to use words like "friend" lightly. They have far fewer "friends" than do people in low context cultures, but their friendships tend to be much deeper, too. There is also less reliance on the written and spoken word; it's the context of how something is said or written that's more important. Japan is a good example of a high context culture.

134. B: One of the primary changes that occurred in the 2006 Pension Protection Act (PPA) is that employers may automatically enroll employees in a 401(k) plan and employees have to choose to opt out. The lowered age limit for vesting was reflected in the Retirement Equity Act (REA) of 1984. The higher income tax applied to part of the pension plan was reflected in the Unemployment Compensation Amendments of 1992. The Economic Growth and Tax Relief Reconciliation Act (EGTERRA) of 2001 enabled employees over the age of 50 to increase their catch-up contributions.

135. B: Edith's employer may discontinue her COBRA coverage if she fails to make a payment within 30 days of the payment due date. COBRA may not be discontinued after only 15 days without a payment. The employer is not obligated to extend COBRA for 45 days or 60 days after a missed payment.

136. D: COBRA coverage is allowed for 36 months after a divorce occurs. The other answer choices—0 months, 18 months, and 29 months—are too brief (or, in the case of 0 months, nonexistent).

137. C: COBRA coverage is provided for 29 months after an employee termination due to being disabled. The options for 0 months and 18 months are too brief; the option for 36 months goes beyond the COBRA provision.

138. D: When a dependent child no longer falls under standard health coverage, he can fall under the COBRA provision for an extra 36 months. The other answer choices—0 months, 18 months, and 29 months—are too brief.

139. A: If employment is terminated due to "gross misconduct," the former employee is not entitled to any COBRA coverage. The other answer choices are too high; the employer has no obligation to support COBRA coverage for the terminated employee.

140. D: In the event of a divorce or legal separation, the employer must be notified within 60 days. An employee may notify the employer well before this—as in 15 days, 30 days, or 45 days—but the employee has a full 60 days to notify the employer.

141. B: A money purchase plan offers employees a fixed annual percentage and thus is best in a company that has fairly consistent annual earnings. A profit-sharing plan, also known as a discretionary contribution plan, is considered to be best in a company that has highly variable annual profits. A cash balance plan is considered "portable" because employees can remove the money from the plan and convert the payment into other forms. A target benefit plan uses actuarial formulas to determine how much an employee will receive toward retirement.

142. A: A profit-sharing plan, also known as a discretionary contribution plan, is considered to be best in a company that has highly variable annual profits. A money purchase plan offers employees a fixed annual percentage and thus is best in a company that has fairly consistent annual earnings. A

cash balance plan is considered "portable" because employees can remove the money from the plan and convert the payment into other forms. A target benefit plan uses actuarial formulas to determine how much an employee will receive toward retirement.

143. C: A cash balance plan is considered "portable" because employees can remove the money from the plan and convert the payment into other forms. A profit-sharing plan, also known as a discretionary contribution plan, is considered to be best in a company that has highly variable annual profits. A money purchase plan offers employees a fixed annual percentage and thus is best in a company that has fairly consistent annual earnings. A target benefit plan uses actuarial formulas to determine how much an employee will receive toward retirement.

144. A: Social Security, state income tax, and federal income tax are considered statutory deductions. Union dues are not considered statutory deductions, although they may be provided for in some states.

145. C: The Department of Labor is responsible for enforcing the rights of veterans in the workplace. The EEOC, DOJ, and OFCCP are all responsible for enforcing other rights within the workplace.

146. D: According to Title III of the Consumer Credit Protection Act of 1968, up to 50 percent of an employee's income may be garnished for child support payments, if the employee is responsible for supporting a child or a spouse. All other answer choices—15 percent, 25 percent, and 35 percent—are too low.

147. B: A representation petition must be completed at least 30 days in advance of a planned union picketing. Failing to submit the petition within this time frame can result in the petition being unrecognized and thus being deemed an unfair labor practice. Among the answer choices, 15 days is obviously too short of a notice, and both 45 days and 60 days exceed the legal expectation. The union may, of course, notify that far in advance, but it is not necessary.

148. C: The President may require a cooling-off period for 80 days, if the strike is deemed to have national consequences. In other words, if the strike has the potential to result in serious consequences to national activities, the President may get involved and require the parties to come together and discuss the issue. The options for 30 days and 50 days are too low, and the option for 100 days is too high. (It should be noted that the President does not have to require the full 80 days, but the full 80 days is provided as an option.)

149. B: The Labor-Management Relations Act (LMRA) of 1947 is also known as the Taft-Hartley Act (or just Taft-Hartley). The Norris-LaGuardia goes by no other name. The Wagner Act is the alternative name for the National Labor Relations Act (NLRA). And the Landrum-Griffith Act is also known as Labor-Management Reporting and Disclosure Act (LMRDA).

150. B: LMRDA required that local unions conduct leadership elections every three years. Answer choice D reflects the requirement for national unions (discussed in question 151). The other answer choices do not reflect union leadership election requirements.

151. D: LMRDA required that national unions conduct leadership elections every five years. As noted in the answer for question 150, the option for three years reflects the requirement for local unions. The other answer choices do not reflect union leadership election requirements.

152. D: As mentioned in the answer for question 149, the Labor-Management Reporting and Disclosure Act (LMRDA) of 1959 also goes by the name of Landrum-Griffith (or the Landrum-

Griffith Act). The Taft-Hartley Act is the alternative name for the Labor-Management Relations Act (LMRA) of 1947. The Norris-LaGuardia goes by no other name. The Wagner Act is the alternative name for the National Labor Relations Act (NLRA).

153. A: Positional bargaining is one among many bargaining options for employers, and entering into positional bargaining is not considered to be an unfair labor practice. However, entering into a hot cargo agreement with the union, taking disciplinary actions against those who participate in unions, and declining to enter into a bargain with the employee union may be considered unfair labor practices for employers.

154. B: Requiring employers to sign a security clause to be part of the union is fairly standard procedure: it protects the union when the time comes for the union to enter into bargaining with the employer. However, preventing an employee from selecting bargaining representation, requiring an employee to continue in a job that is technologically obsolete, and declining to enter into good faith negotiations with the employer may be considered unfair labor practices for unions.

155. D: A labor charge must be filed within 6 months of an incident. The charge may, of course, be filed within 3, 4, or 5 months, but these options do not reflect the full legal provision.

156. C: Before submitting to the employer a demand for recognition, the labor union must acquire signed authorization cards from employees. This essentially provides an official statement from employees about their intent to unionize and lets the NLRB know that unionizing activity has support from employees. Petitioning the NLRB for voluntary recognition occurs next. Establishing a bargaining position and meeting with the employer to discuss alternatives are activities of the union itself, but they are not part of the actual unionization process.

157. B: Salting occurs when someone takes a job with a company that the union has targeted for employee unionization, and thus works to encourage employees at the new company to organize a union. This would be viewed as a form of instigation and is thus not a fair labor practice. Wildcatting, per se, does not exist, although there is a *wildcat strike*, which occurs in spite of a contractual prohibition against strikes. Featherbedding refers to the activity of keeping an employee in a position despite that position being considered obsolete due to changes in technology. And leafleting is a union activity that involves passing out leaflets about the union's position and thus drumming up support.

158. C: A "petitional" form of picketing does not exist. The recognized forms of picketing are as follows: organizational, informational, and recognitional.

159. C: The employer's decision is voluntary, and thus a voluntary-recognition election bar will result, preventing the labor union from conducting elections in the immediate future. A prior-petition bar results when the union withdraws an election request petition and then resubmits it. A certification-year bar results when the NLRB has recently recognized and certified a representative for bargaining on behalf of the union. A blocking-charge bar occurs when an unfair labor practice charge remains pending.

160. D: As indicated in the answer for question 160, a blocking-charge bar occurs when an unfair labor practice charge remains pending. Since this is the case in the scenario provided, the blocking-charge bar will apply. A prior-petition bar results when the union withdraws an election request petition and then resubmits it. A certification-year bar results when the NLRB has recently recognized and certified a representative for bargaining on behalf of the union. A voluntary-recognition bar occurs when the employer voluntarily recognizes the union as the primary bargaining unit for employees.

161. B: Integrative bargaining results when the different sides agree to compromise on certain issues by taking the big picture into account. Positional bargaining results when each side establishes a clear position and aims to achieve the goal or goals of that position. Interest-based bargaining results when both sides acknowledge that they have a strong motivation in the continuity of business activities, and thus proceed in negotiations with this acknowledgement. Distributive bargaining is another name for positional bargaining.

162. C: Interest-based bargaining results when both sides acknowledge that they have a strong motivation in the continuity of business activities, and thus proceed in negotiations with this acknowledgement. Positional bargaining results when each side establishes a clear position and aims to achieve the goal or goals of that position. Integrative bargaining results when the different sides agree to compromise on certain issues by taking the big picture into account. Distributive bargaining is another name for positional bargaining.

163. D: Positional bargaining is also known as hard bargaining (and sometimes as distributive bargaining). Integrative bargaining is a form or principled bargaining. Coordinated bargaining is not a recognized collective bargaining position.

164. C: Pattern bargaining, whipsawing, and leapfrogging are all alternate names for parallel bargaining. Single-unit bargaining has no alternate names. Multi-employer bargaining also has no recognized alternate names. Multi-unit bargaining is also known as coordinated bargaining.

165. D: Among the criteria under which the NLRB recognizes a successor employer, or a new employer who has taken over a company, are the following: indicating a significant continuity in standard business activities, establishing a clear agreement with the previous employer, and demonstrating a clear parallel in the products and procedures of the company. The NLRB also recognizes as a successor employer one who assimilates a reasonable number of employees from under the previous employer, but the successor employer is not necessarily expected to assimilate *all* employees.

166. D: Employee retirement plans still in force. From the Department of Labor website: "The Form 5500 Series is an important compliance, research, and disclosure tool for the Department of Labor, a disclosure document for plan participants and beneficiaries, and a source of information and data for use by other Federal agencies, Congress, and the private sector in assessing employee benefit, tax, and economic trends and policies."

167. D: Noncompete agreement. Retirement plans, collective bargaining agreements, and executive employment contracts all represent potential legal and financial obligations another firm may not desire to take upon itself. However, any company that wants to divest itself of a less profitable division should have no problem signing an agreement not to compete with the firm that takes the division off its hands.

168. B: Maturity. During the startup, there is generally little hiring, and there is very little time or money for training. Most employees will do several jobs. During the growth phase, things are starting to settle down, but there still isn't much training. In the decline phase, companies usually aren't doing much hiring or training, as the company's prospects are going downhill.

169. B: An employee has 90 days to file a complaint with OSHA regarding retaliation from an employer for exposing a company violation. The other answer choices are either too low (60 days) or too high (120 days and 180 days).

170. D: In response to the employee's filing, OSHA then has 180 days to issue a final order against the employer. The other answer choices (60 days, 90 days, and 120 days) are too low.

171. B: If OSHA fails to issue the final order, the employee then has the right to file a law suit in a U.S. district court. The employee may choose to contact his congressional representative, but it is more than likely the representative will simply review the employee's legal rights and encourage filing suit. Requesting a restraining order is not necessarily an appropriate step in this case; filing the full law suit, however, is. Submitting an official request about an improvement to the whistleblower policy is unlikely to accomplish much; the employer's actions would call for a larger response from OSHA and the legal system.

172. C: OSHA's first goal is to attempt a reconciliation between the employee and his employer. If there is a possibility of avoiding legal action, it should be taken to avoid weighing down the legal system. (Thus answer choice B is not correct.) In the process of this reconciliation, OSHA might also work to have the employee reinstated with full benefits and back pay, but this would reflect the individual situation and is part of the larger reconciliation process instead of the primary goal. OSHA could step in to protect the employee by requiring continued pay without requiring a return to work, but again this would reflect an individual situation and would not necessarily be the primary goal.

173. A: The Department of Justice is responsible for enforcing privacy laws. The other agencies listed—the EEOC, the FTC, and the DOL—are all responsible for enforcing other laws that apply to the employer-employee relationship.

174. B: The updated changes to the Equal Employment Opportunity Act of 1972 specifically included educational institutions, federal government, and state and local government. Labor unions were not listed among these updated legal applications in 1972.

175. B: Quite a bit higher. Getting people to move to foreign countries to live and work takes a lot of money. It also takes a lot to keep them happy enough to stay there and to enable them to do their job well. Generally speaking, the total compensation for an expatriate may be two to three times that of a similar employee in the states.

Thank You

We at Mometrix would like to extend our heartfelt thanks to you, our friend and patron, for allowing us to play a part in your journey. It is a privilege to serve people from all walks of life who are unified in their commitment to building the best future they can for themselves.

The preparation you devote to these important testing milestones may be the most valuable educational opportunity you have for making a real difference in your life. We encourage you to put your heart into it—that feeling of succeeding, overcoming, and yes, conquering will be well worth the hours you've invested.

We want to hear your story, your struggles and your successes, and if you see any opportunities for us to improve our materials so we can help others even more effectively in the future, please share that with us as well. **The team at Mometrix would be absolutely thrilled to hear from you!** So please, send us an email (support@mometrix.com) and let's stay in touch.

If you feel as though you need additional help, please check out the other resources we offer:

Study Guide: http://MometrixStudyGuides.com/HRCI

Flashcards: http://MometrixFlashcards.com/HRCI